LOVE IN TWO LANGUAGES

LOVE IN TWO LANGUAGES

Lessons on Mothering
in a Culture of Individuality

Bonnie Ohye

Bonnie Ohye, Ph.D.

A Living Press Planet Book

VIKING

VIKING
Published by the Penguin Group
Penguin Putnam Inc., 375 Hudson Street, New York, New York 10014, U.S.A.
Penguin Books Ltd, 27 Wrights Lane, London W8 5TZ, England
Penguin Books Australia Ltd, Ringwood, Victoria, Australia
Penguin Books Canada Ltd., 10 Alcorn Avenue, Toronto, Ontario, Canada M4V 3B2
Penguin Books (N.Z.) Ltd, 182–190 Wairau Road, Auckland 10, New Zealand

Penguin Books Ltd, Registered Offices:
Harmondsworth, Middlesex, England

First published in 2001 by Viking Penguin,
a member of Penguin Putnam Inc.

10 9 8 7 6 5 4 3 2 1

Grateful acknowledgment is made for permission to reprint the following copyrighted
works:

   Excerpt from "The Map" from *The Collected Poems 1927–1979* by Elizabeth Bishop.
Copyright © 1979, 1983 by Alice Helen Methfessel. Reprinted by permission of Farrar,
Straus & Giroux, LLC.
   "Water" by Christopher Jane Corkery. Copyright © 1979 by The Antioch Review,
Inc. First appeared in *The Antioch Review,* vol. 37, no. 4. Reprinted by permission of the
editors.
   Excerpt from "Wartime" from *Tipping Point* by Fred Marchant. Copyright © 1993 by
Fred Marchant. Reprinted by permission of the author and The Word Works.
   Excerpt from "Crossing the Atlantic" and draft of "Little Girl, My Stringbean, My
Lovely Woman" from *Anne Sexton: A Self-Portrait in Letters,* edited by Linda Gray Sexton
and Lois Ames. Copyright © 1977 by Linda Gray Sexton and Loring Conant, Jr., execu-
tors of the will of Anne Sexton. Reprinted by permission of Houghton Mifflin Co. All
rights reserved.

Library of Congress Cataloging-in-Publication Data
Ohye, Bonnie.
   Love in two languages : lessons on mothering in a culture of individuality / Bonnie
Ohye.
       p.   cm.
   "A Living press planet book."
   ISBN 0-670-88773-0
      1. Mother and child. 2. Mothers—Psychology. 3. Love, Maternal. I. Title.
BF723.M55 O37 2001
306.874'3—dc21   2001017556

This book is printed on acid-free paper. ∞

Printed in the United States of America
Set in Garamond 3 with Martin Gothic
Designed by Carla Bolte

For my daughters,

and in memory of my mother,

Teruko Hayashi Ohye

We cannot be as water always.
Cannot fall graceful
Over treacherous rocks
continuous to the pool below,
always heading home, always
having arrived there, no space
between the changes and the self . . .

We cannot be as water always
but only on occasion,
the graceless hands turned up,
revealing grace, the tongue
once mute, released,
and yielding for a moment
what the heart had always felt.

—Christopher Jane Corkery, from "Water"

CONTENTS

LESSONS ON SUSPENDING OUR DESIRES

PREFACE

The Language of Attentive Love

In the eyes of the world, I became a mother on January 2, 1986 at 8:25 A.M. when my first daughter Emily was born. I was thirty-three years old and most would say as well prepared as anyone could be for motherhood. I was trained as a child psychologist at the Harvard Medical School, where I currently teach young psychologists and psychiatrists about working with troubled children and their parents. In childhood and adolescence I was not only surrounded by, but in charge of, babies and younger children. I had three younger siblings and four younger cousins, and lived in a southern California neighborhood where mothers and their children flowed into and out of each other's homes freely and comfortably. By the time I was thirteen, I had a namesake, the second cousin of a neighborhood girlfriend, a delicate little baby with wild black hair and beautiful dark eyes.

———

Before I had children of my own, it seemed a great advantage that I was a child psychologist, well versed in the prevailing ideas about what parents must do to rear happy and healthy children. Since helping mothers and fathers to be better parents is what my work is about, it seemed all I had to do was put into practice what I advise others to do. Instead, I found myself rethinking convictions firmly held and concepts that I believed I understood so thoroughly; revisiting them, no longer abstractly or purely academically, but through my real and passionate and ever changing, yet sometimes struggling, relationships to my two children.

As I became aware that the dilemmas mothers face are far more complex and multilayered than I could ever have suspected, I started to see mothers—friends, patients, myself—in a different light. I began to appreciate that many of the ideas about what children need from their mothers, ideas that seemed so straightforward before I became a mother *(protect them . . . be firm . . . give them their independence . . . be warm . . . love them just the same)* felt incomplete or simplistic when I came face-to-face with children of my own.

My education and training had provided me with a rich and powerful language to describe a child's development. And life experience made me familiar with hugs, kisses, lullabies and bedtime stories, all those precious moments of feeling close and brimming over with affection and love for a child. But what neither my training nor life had prepared me fully for were all those moments in a mother's day that are not simply one or the other, all the moments that require both a mother's heart and a mother's mind, knowledge and intuition, joined together.

We are introduced naturally to this kind of mothering as our babies, tiny strangers at first, make themselves known to us, their patterns of eating and sleeping, the signs of hunger or fatigue that a stranger would miss, gradually becoming familiar and unmistakable. It continues as we understand our toddler well enough to figure out that if the water in the tub is more than two inches high, he will refuse to climb in; and so we make do with an inch instead. Or when harried, we come upon a muddy trail of footprints stamped like lily pads across the living room rug, and want to scream. But because we glimpse our daughter's muddy boots, side by side, military in their neatness by the back door, right where we have told her to put them a million times, we take a deep breath and find the words to praise, not scold.

Once, I would have described the mother who did not scold her child with the muddy boots as "patient," not loving. I thought the word "sensitive" described thoroughly the mother who hears the quaver in her fourth grader's voice as he reports his school day was "fine," and in spite of her wish to make it better, waits until bedtime to hear more. But the longer I am a mother, the more certain I am that in these minute exchanges between a mother and child, moments that go unheralded because they are not spontaneous or carefree, we are speaking to our children in a profoundly necessary, though less celebrated language of love.

Recognizing this other language of love, one that places the nurture of a close and trusting relationship between mother and child at the fore, can be an unexpected challenge, for it is often eclipsed by the more vigorous and clamorous language of "optimizing" our children's development. Until I could name this second language and discover it had a vocabulary all its own, I would often lose sight of it, and find myself questioning its importance. *Love in Two Languages* grows out of my wish to articulate the language of a mother's intuitive understanding of a child, and the private and public forces that so often cause mothers to lose sight of its value.

I suspect I was drawn to the task of describing this quietly eloquent language of love, a counterpoint to the one of my academic education, in part because as a third-generation Japanese American I have lived between two cultures and their different idioms of expression. Growing up both within and outside of the mainstream has given me an appreciation for things less visible in our culture and a good deal of practice in knitting differences together, not as conflicted dualities, but in comfortable and respectful coexistence. Although as a teenager I chafed at this place in the social landscape of "standing on two shores at once," it has served well as a starting point for this exploration of a less visible kind of love.

———

Philosopher Sara Ruddick has described this kind of love as attentive or clear-sighted. It is love with many facets. Most essentially, it is love that moves a mother to see a child as he or she truly is, and to accept the person that she sees. Because it is clear-sighted, it permits a mother to form an accurate understanding of her child, not one constructed out of her fantasies, wishes and needs. It is an understanding of a child not driven primarily by a mother's desire to "[find] herself in him." Although similar, attentive love is not identical to empathy. For when a mother loves a child clear-sightedly, she aspires to understand what he feels not only when she recognizes herself in his experience, but also, and with equal interest, when she does not. When a mother is attentively loving she asks a child, "What are you going through?" As Ruddick describes it, she will "wait to hear the answer rather than giving it. She learns to ask again and keep listening even if she cannot make sense of what she hears or can barely tolerate the child she has understood."

Love that requires us to listen, to look, and to understand and accept before acting, is a demanding kind of love. Fortunately, our children do not need constant loving attention. Like driving a winding mountain road, there are times our children require us to be more attentive. When the road narrows or the fog rolls in, we instinctively tighten our grip on the steering wheel, sit up straight and concentrate. Eventually, the hairpin turns ease, the road opens and widens and we relax. The demand to think only about driving recedes, and we are free to return to what we were thinking and doing before.

Like driving, loving children attentively does not require special gifts. All that is required is a receptive attitude and a willingness to put aside our concerns and pay close and undivided attention. But because the world is imperfect, and we are too, there are the inevitable bumps in the road. There are times we are too distracted to be wholly attentive. Many of these impediments to attentive love spring from ideas about good children and good mothers, ideas that we have taken to heart long before we become mothers ourselves. Some feel so natural and irrefutable they could have been given to us in the air that we breathe. I do not think it necessary, or maybe even possible, to rid ourselves of these ideas, only to become more aware of them, alert to their subtle guises and their influence on our relationships to our children. For instance, I have a new appreciation and respect for my friend who grates the cheese her four-year-old son takes for snack because he says his mouth has not "grown up yet," even though the judgment in her own mother's question, "Are you still doing that for him?" lingers in her thoughts.

Bringing the idea of attentive love more fully into my work as a therapist and relationships with my children has opened a door to a new understanding of what children need and what good mothers do. Mothers need to do more than love children attentively, of course. We must protect and nurture and teach them, too. But I am convinced that if we allow our acts of protection, nurture and instruction to be guided by the principle of attentive love, we gradually acquire a way to disentangle and quiet the disparate voices that tell us how to be good mothers. As we make decisions and choices on our children's behalf not in response to the romanticized and idealized visions of the ideal mother and her ideal child, but out of a closely observed, ever deepening and articulate understanding of our very own unique, delightful and exasperating, demanding and exuberant children, we not only build relationships with our children that are filled with trust, but become more confident in ourselves as mothers.

———

Loving a child attentively won't guarantee he will achieve his milestones on time, or guarantee that she will enjoy future academic, social or athletic success. It does, however, do something I believe is infinitely more valuable. It paves the way to a close, honest and sturdy relationship with your child; a relationship that children do not fear depends on being someone other than who they really are to be loved and accepted. It brings forth relationships with children that are cherished for their mutual respect and genuine understanding. By loving clear-sightedly, we become mothers our children trust, and turn to, over a lifetime.

Love in Two Languages sets out my observations and reflections on what it means to love children attentively. Fathers as well as mothers can and do love children attentively. Expressing clear-sighted love is not something only mothers do. It does seem, however, that the cultural expectation for the sensitivity and emotional receptivity intrinsic to attentive love is placed more squarely and inexorably in the province of mothers, and the psychological workings of that demand play out more acutely and particularly for them. Consequently, the themes of a mother "listening to her child," a mother "looking at her child," and a mother "suspending her own desires in the face of her child's needs" organize my observations of the interplay of heart and mind in the work of clear-sighted love. I have come to think of this triad as the vocabulary in the language of a mother's loving attention. Although I have separated these three elements from one another, I do so cautiously, aware that in the moments when a mother loves clear-sightedly, she does not just listen, or just look or suspend her desires, but does all three.

Mothers need affirmation of their perception that nurturing sound, trusting relationships with children is often difficult in our individualistic culture, with its emphasis on separation rather than connection, on immediate success rather than steady, sure maturation, and on emotional toughness rather than emotional sensitivity and human vulnerability. By joining the lessons that my patients, friends and children have taught me about attentive love with ideas and scholarship on child development, I hope to give mothers an intellectual foothold that supports that awareness. It is a foothold that not only grounds the development of an emotionally accurate understanding of a child, but also enables mothers to stand firm in the face of cultural messages that fail to reflect its importance.

In this regard, I describe, for example, research on the

question of why the patterns of our earliest relationships recur in our relationships to our children, on temperamental differences in children and their effect on mothers, on the complex issue of boys, their activity level and aggression, and nontraditional notions about identity, ones that capture more accurately the evolution of one's sense of self as a mother. Although I am a psychologist, I have found historical, sociological and cultural writings on motherhood enormously illuminating. Where relevant, I have drawn from them to show that the origins of the ideas that can interfere with a mother's expression of attentive love are many times located not in the mother's psyche, but in the legacy of views of mothers we inherit without even knowing it. I hope this broadening of perspective offers reassurance and a sense of relief. By including these views I also wish to suggest that the cultural prescriptions mothers labor under are not immutable and universal. They are open to question and active revision in relationship to one's child.

For many months I wrestled with the question of how personal this book should be. My academic training taught me to eschew the subjective. So at first I did try to adhere to this standard, scrupulously avoiding anything personal. But I found that book to be unlike the one in my deepest imaginings. Gradually I realized the book I wanted to write is the one I wish I had had myself—a book that would invite contemplation and speak to the dilemmas of mothering in a culture of individuality. Exploring these tensions, I have tried to stay true to a mother's experience. I have tried to resist telling false, though perhaps more comfortable versions of these stories of love, portraits that would edit out a mother's hesitation, doubt and effort as she attempts the indirect and sometimes uncertain course of loving children clear-sightedly.

Love in Two Languages is a book about the challenges and satisfactions of embracing a view of mothering that encompasses not only the nurture of a child's individual development, but also the nurture of a strong, resilient, and honest relationship between mother and child, as well. It examines the powerful, and sometimes corrosive, influence our culture's imperatives about good mothers and good children exert on a mother's wish for such a relationship. And it looks in equal measure at how the complexity of who we are as women, women with our own stories, foibles, passions, secrets and paths not taken, can interfere with this maternal ideal. I hope that by speaking honestly, sharing many stories from my own family as well as stories from friends and patients, others who are engaged in the profound journey of becoming mothers will see themselves, and find herein moments of clarity, renewal and friendship.

LESSONS ON LISTENING

. . . even her silence was a kind of speech.

Susan Griffin, *A Chorus of Stones*

ECHOES

Our Mothers' Stories

"Is this you, Mommy? Or is it *your* mommy? You two have the *same* chubby cheeks!" My six-year-old daughter Rachel's eyes are twinkling mischievously as she holds out an old black-and-white photograph for me to look at. The picture is of my mother when she was an infant. She is dressed in a long white baptismal gown, starched and voluminous, no hint of the chubby arms and legs underneath, just a round full face gazing steadily out at the world. In my thirteen-year-old daughter Emily's words, "open and unafraid." This picture is still in its original paper frame, now a faded putty gray. The name of the place where it was taken, Jackson Studios, is stamped in gold letters on the front. It is a lovely photograph. I like its shape, long and slender, like a Japanese scroll. It is the only one I have ever seen of my mother as a baby, most everything of sentimental value had to be left behind when her family was relocated in World War II. My uncle Jack found the picture when he was sorting through some old boxes in my grandparents' house last year. He had never seen it before either and marveled that my grandparents had been able to afford to have it taken.

———

My mother, Teruko, was born in Seattle, but grew up on a small island in the Puget Sound ten miles northwest of Seattle. Today the island is among the most desirable places in suburban Seattle to live. Every morning, professional-looking men and women commute to work by ferry poised over their laptops and steaming cups of coffee; and in the evening as they make the return trip, they can sip a glass of wine and watch the setting sun. But when my mother was a child, the island was considered an isolated, rural location, known for small berry farms like the one my grandparents owned. The fourth of eight children, she had two sisters and five brothers. One of her younger brothers died as a toddler when he fell into an abandoned well near the family farm. As a three-year-old she too almost drowned when a rotted plank on a bridge gave way and she dropped into the icy water below. To this day her sister Mary's voice tightens and then fills with relief as she talks about the man who came along at the right time to save her little sister. It is clear as she recounts this accident that that stranger's appearance felt like a miracle to her. To have Rachel holding this piece of

my past, once lost, now recovered, is something of a miracle of its very own.

My mother had four children, half as many children as
her mother. And I have half that number again. She reared
my sister, brothers and me without a husband, supported
in her single parenthood by the love and generosity of my
grandparents and aunts and uncles. My grandparents provided childcare; one of my aunts gave us all our haircuts,
and she gave my sister and me our Toni permanent waves
at Easter; my uncles cheerfully took us on excursions to
the zoo and on shopping trips at Christmastime. Unlike
my mother, I am not raising my children alone, but with
a husband who is a devoted and involved father. My children do not have their grandparents, aunts, uncles and
cousins nearby as I did, but are nurtured by a strong and
loving circle of friends and neighbors. Yet, beneath these
differences in outward circumstance, my mother and I can
seem to me as alike as two peas in a pod. Most women I
know feel like this at one time or another. There are those
times when our actions toward our children are reflected
back to us, as though in a mirror, and like Rachel, we begin to wonder, "Which one am I really?"

For years, my friend Gloria claimed she had achieved her
life's objective of being someone completely unlike her
mother. She pointed to her successful career, her com-
manding position in her corporation as the antithesis of
her mother's passivity and subordination to her husband.
She promised herself her whole childhood that she would

be the model of strength and independence her mother was not. She would do this for her children.

One night Gloria phoned very upset. Her son Joe had just stormed up the stairs, angry and shouting at her that he wanted to be left alone. Gloria explained that Joe had been rinsing his dinner dishes at the kitchen sink when she walked in from the dining room. To her horror, she saw the same vacant, slack-jawed expression on Joe's face that she nightly rebuked her own mother for. She yelled at Joe to "wipe that awful look" from his face. She couldn't believe what she had done. And she couldn't believe she was telling me about this. But she was exhausted from her long day at work, and she could not stop herself. The irritation, disappointment and anger she had tried to sidestep all her life came welling up, spilling over into her relationship to her son. Gloria was afraid that like her mother, she was pushing a child away.

I suppose there are mothers on this earth who are so transformed by their love for a child that they can keep their own childhood stories from interfering with their relationship with their sons and daughters. But for most of us, it is most inescapably with our children that we are reminded, sometimes gently, sometimes rudely, of who we are, and of the circumstances and people from the past with whom we remain most intimately connected. We discover that we are not only kind, generous, playful and lovingly attentive, but can be petty, impatient, domineering, arbitrary and neglectful, as well. We come face-to-face with the parts of ourselves we struggle mightily to deny, and to our dismay, we can catch ourselves re-creating un-comfortable, and even painful aspects of our significant relationships from the past.

―――

Unlike my friend Gloria, most of the time, I don't mind if I am like my mother. She was a much loved elementary school teacher, admired for her ability to teach young children how to read, her warm, sunny disposition and her quietly busy classrooms. Always prepared, rarely ruffled or frantic, she emanated a calm, unflappable presence. Few who knew her would have described her as anxious. And yet, although she never directly said to me, "The world is a dangerous place. I fear for your safety," I knew she felt that way. She was never dramatic or hysterical. Neither was she the kind of mother who told hair-raising tales about children who had been hurt, calling our attention to the news reports of children who were missing or abducted or maimed. I just knew, without her having to say so, that she worried that something terrible could happen to one of us.

When I was a teenager, I took pride in the fact that her apprehensiveness hadn't made me a fearful or an anxious child. I hadn't had nightmares of monsters in the closet or under my bed, and wasn't a child who refused to separate from her mother. But somehow I knew I should never do anything that would make her fearful about me. I should play it safe. It's not hard to guess that it can be tough to experiment and be adventurous if you feel your mother's anxiety hovering around you. Children need to test themselves. They need to take risks in order to figure out who they are. And if they can't, they will usually figure out a way to do it anyway. I loved my mother, and I didn't want to fill her with dread. But I also wanted to do the things growing children do. I found the way I could do that, yet spare my mother was to say, "It's a school-related activity." I managed to do quite a bit using this strategy, and by the time I moved to Boston in my mid-twenties, I prided myself on my independence. I believed I had been untouched by my mother's worry.

Then I had my first baby and all the monsters that were never under my childhood bed suddenly appeared under my baby's. But I didn't actually feel my anxiety, I took action instead. I did what therapists call turning passive into active. I adopted the motto, "Be prepared." As a new mother, being prepared took the form of stocking the trunk of my car with emergency baby supplies. I took all my worry about the world and put it into a diaper bag and put the bag in the trunk of my car. It was a first-aid kit against calamity: A & D ointment, Tylenol, Band-Aids, diaper wipes and extra diapers, a change of clothes (a *complete* change of clothes, including hat, mittens and jacket in the winter months, sunscreen and hat in the summer months, socks and slippers), tiny garbage bags (for the dirty diapers), receiving blanket and a baby bottle. The most important item, however, was technically not in the bag. It was in the glove compartment, a pair of scissors. I needed them because I had read somewhere that a child had choked to death when the carseat harness retracted and the mother couldn't loosen it in time. I wasn't taking any chances that could happen to me and to my baby.

I realize now I was being a little nutty. But it felt absolutely necessary then. That bag had to be in the trunk of my car. I never once noticed that none of my friends with infants found it necessary to have such a bag. Never once noticed that even without such a bag, bulging with charms against evil, their babies were quite happy and healthy and safe. That's because I was too busy being just like my mother, in exactly the way I most wanted not to be, worried.

Fortunately for my children, I've gained some perspective on this bit of my maternal legacy. I understand that in my own motherhood, I translated my mother's silent message, "Don't go out there" to "When you go, be prepared." Sometimes I wonder what it will be in the next generation. In the meantime, I am determined to get and keep a grip on my little problem with worrying because it's hard on children to grow up feeling they must protect parents from feeling anxious or fearful. There is, however, one chink in the dike of my resolve: dressing them in winter. Like clockwork, this worry creeps up on me as the days shorten and the first chilly autumn nights leave frost on the windowpanes. It surges forward and pushes itself through that small hole and nags at me, and nags at my children. I know I am in its grip when I feel myself stiffen as I notice Emily hasn't bothered to dry her hair before going to school, and it's twenty degrees outside. Our New England–born and bred neighbors don't bat an eye. They did it; their children did it; no one died of pneumonia. Even with their good-humored chuckling ringing in my ears, I am nevertheless driven every year to buy my girls the most cold-resistant, heavy-duty snow boots I can find. Yanking them onto her feet, Rachel, who runs like the wind, complains bitterly to me that she is always "it" when she plays tag at recess. It's no wonder. Her boots are like bricks. Those are merely the external signs. The list running in my head, a toy train on its circular track, is endless: mittens, hat, neck warmer, lip balm, tissues. I used to tell myself my precautions were not because I was an anxious mother, but because I hadn't grown up where it was cold and snowy in the winter. I told myself that I was lacking an inbred gauge that other moms seemed to possess. This is, of course, just a fancy way of disguising the fact that I worry, just like my mother.

I know that I have to let my children out, even in winter. I have to back off when they say, "I'm okay, Mom." I have to bite my tongue and try not to say anything at all. I am very lucky. Emily and Rachel are patient with me. I say, "Don't forget . . ." "Did you remember to . . . ?" They sigh. Their shoulders, Emily's strong, athletic ones, Rachel's slight, knobby ones, rise gently up, then down, as they stand at the threshold of the door ready to rush out to whatever wonderful adventure awaits them. One day, although I cannot tell you why I did this, I showed them the first winter coat I ever bought after moving East, eighteen years ago. It had been shoved into the farthest reaches of a spare closet. It is army green, very long, and is so heavily padded it is stiff enough to stand up on its own, like a suit of armor. The hood has a drawstring with massive toggles. The visor is constructed so that it bends in so far that, if you do it right, it obliterates from view everything except the eyes. I put it on for the girls. I think it was the middle of July. And even though they are usually quite well mannered children, they were laughing *at* me so hard they were staggering around, clutching their bellies, gasping for air. It was wonderful.

———

It does seem, whether we feel comfortable with the idea or not, that our families have a lot to do with the kind of mothers we become. In those first bonds, we learn how close relationships are supposed to work, and how they feel. We learn what love and being cared for feel like. I am thinking here not only that some families hug and kiss and others do not. I am thinking of the intimate exchanges that have private meanings often understood uniquely within one's family. My friend Rosa and her father come to mind. Rosa's first baby was very seriously ill when he was born. He is a very healthy and energetic six-year-old now, but at the time there was a great deal of uncertainty about whether he would live or not. When Rosa's parents arrived at the hospital during the first days of this crisis, her physician father entered her room, quickly pecked her on the cheek, settled himself in the chair next to her bed and promptly fell asleep. Rosa felt immediately reassured seeing her father napping peacefully. She understood that if her father had grave concerns about her son, he would not be able to sleep. His napping, a reaction an outside observer might interpret as callous or coldhearted, was experienced by Rosa as comforting instead.

Exactly how this learning happens is one of the most intriguing questions in psychology. Some theories suggest we adopt behaviors and attitudes that are reinforced and we fail to acquire those that are not. Some explanations involve templates, scripts and schemata of family relationships. Others invoke places in the brain, in cells, neurons and neurotransmitters, where images, memories and patterns of our early experience of being cared for might be stored.

All of these possibilities are compelling in their own right. Each explains how some aspects of the patterns of our family relationships continue from one generation to the next. Of these, I have been most interested in those notions that clarify the interior world of our relationships to our children, like the reality that was created between my friend Gloria and her son Joe. One such idea is the psychoanalytic concept of "repetition," another is a concept from attachment theory, the "internal working model."

Early in his exploration of psychoanalytic technique, Freud noted that the pattern of our earliest relationships recurs in our close relationships later in life. He called this phenomenon "repeating." Freud wrote, "The patient does not *remember* anything of what he has forgotten and repressed, but acts it out. He reproduces it not as a memory, but as an action; he *repeats* it, without, of course, knowing that he is repeating it."

Freud developed the concept of repeating by observing that if he refrained from allowing his patients to know about him—his opinions, tastes and beliefs—they not only spoke to him of emotional conflict in current relationships, but reenacted the same patterns of emotions in relationship to him. They reported feeling toward him as they had felt toward their significant caretaking figures, in most cases, their parents. In "transferring" these thoughts and feelings to Freud, the analyst, patients re-created in a remarkably exact fashion the nature of their early relationships, no matter how unsatisfactory and harmful they might have been. Freud believed that by pointing out the ways the patient unconsciously misinterpreted the analyst's motivations and character to be like those of her original caretakers, psychological distress could be relieved. This process he called "insight."

In classical psychoanalysis, repeating is considered to be an unconscious defense against painful feelings about traumatic childhood experiences, a way to keep unpleasant memories out of awareness. In later developments in psychoanalytic theory, the concept of trauma was revised. Trauma was no longer a single overwhelming event as Freud originally proposed. Rather, small, repetitive acts of parental insensitivity can be traumatic, experienced and remembered as emotionally wounding.

For example, a woman named Linda began therapy because she felt she was no longer in love with her husband. Attracted initially to his sensitivity and expressiveness, she gradually experienced this quality as unbearably childish, and a sign of weakness. She was convinced she needed to divorce her husband in order to be happy. At first, Linda conducted herself as a supremely competent woman, and periodically raised doubts about whether I was being helpful to her. But over the course of our work together, we noted her wish to be both close to and distant and aloof from me. Linda gradually became aware of her fear that I would abandon her just as her warm, but emotionally self-absorbed mother had repeatedly done in search of a wealthy husband. Linda realized she was responding emotionally *as if* I were like her mother. This understanding gained in the therapeutic relationship allowed her to consider her feelings about her husband in a new light, as an unconscious repetition of her feelings about her mother.

———

Although Freud arrived at his ideas about repetition from his work with patients in psychoanalysis, we know from observations of everyday life that this re-creation of our earliest patterns of relationships is not limited to the relationship between client and therapist. We might know someone, a co-worker for example, whose relationships in the office are often tense because she competes fiercely for recognition from her manager much like siblings vie for their parents' attention. Or we know the person who procrastinates completing his part of a project until the last moment because he perceives any demand from an authority figure as unreasonable, and his private struggle with a tyrannical mother becomes public in the work-place.

Later analytic theorists broadened Freud's original formulation of repetition as a form of emotional self-protection. These interpretations emphasized a different aspect of repeating all together. They emphasized repeat-ing as a form of emotional connection, a means of sustain-ing our ties to those who loved us first. "The memory of the early interactions between child and caregiver are re-peated in an effort toward mastery," psychoanalyst Fred Pine writes, ". . . and because of the longings and gratifi-cations the person associates with them." Repeating occurs not only to keep unpleasant memories out of awareness, but also to keep the intense feelings of our first love rela-tionships, pleasure, sadness, elation, anger, among them, alive.

———

One rainy November night in a noisy French restaurant in Los Angeles over twenty years ago, my friend Ellen's mother Margaret told me the story of her childhood. She was close to sixty, but even at sixty, it was quite easy to imagine her the beautiful, determined, emotionally dis-tant mother who inhabited my friend Ellen's childhood memories. Unexpectedly alone when Ellen excused her-self to make a call, Margaret spoke to me with an urgency I did not understand at the time.

She told me she had been born in Dublin between the two world wars, the third of eight children, and the eldest girl. When she was four her parents sent her to live with her father's oldest sister and her husband. A childless couple, they could feed and clothe her when her parents could not, but they did so unhappily. Although Margaret's presence gave them the appearance of being a family, in the privacy of their home they gave no sign of feeling anything toward her other than "Christian obligation." She prayed every night for her parents' circumstances to change so she could return, but she never did.

Once a year on Christmas Day, she visited with her parents and her brothers and sisters. What she remembered most about those holiday reunions was how rudely her brothers and sisters stared at her. Envious, they whispered among themselves, "Why her?" and renamed her "Lucky." It stuck, and after a while only her mother spoke to her by her given name. Soon after turning eighteen, she moved to the United States.

When Margaret married she was intent on having no more children than she and her husband could comfortably provide for. They had three, Ellen and her two brothers, Michael and Ned. Margaret described them as "devoted to me," something she told me she could not understand. She remarked, "By modern standards I was not a very 'understanding' mother. My children would bring their disappointments, frustrations and sorrows to me, asking for comfort and reassurance. I found that extremely trying. Oh, I was very good at appearing to listen to their woes, but all the while, inwardly, I regarded their hardships as laughably inconsequential when compared to those of my girlhood. I have always thought I am living proof that children can grow up just fine without love.

"Three children is an awkward number. Someone is forever feeling left out. Each one of my children thinks he or she is the outsider in our close-knit family. They would never guess I know this about them, but I do. Each believes the other two are closer to me, and each has found a personal shortcoming to explain this state of exclusion. I've always thought that rather dim for such bright youngsters. You would think they could see that the fault is not in them, but in me. It is as though there is a nick inside me somewhere. Like a nick in a phonograph record, it tugs at the sweet melody as it spins innocently toward you, pulling it back into those shiny black vinyl grooves, over, and over, and over again."

———

Seated at a window table, a torrential rain falling outside, I had watched the expressions on Margaret's lovely face appear and disappear. She looked sad, wistful, amused, annoyed. I was taken aback by her candor and the complexity of her story. At twenty-three, I was accustomed to tales of mothers and children in which good and evil are clear and unambiguous. This was different. There had been good and loving intentions all around. I felt indescribably sad for everyone, my sympathies a huge jumble. I was sad for the little girl who missed her family, sad for her brothers and sisters, the parents, the aunt and uncle, but most of all, for the three children who had to navigate the contradiction between their mother's receptivity and the undercurrent of rebuff.

For all my sympathy for Margaret, at twenty-three I believed that *as a mother* she should have been able to transcend her past for the sake of her children. I am very certain I was never told to expect this of mothers; and I'm not even sure when this notion took hold in my mind. I just know it was there, inside me, an assumption taken in from the culture around us. I thought that just like the mother of supermarket tabloids who rescues her child from certain death by lifting a three-ton truck with her bare hands, so should Margaret's love for Ellen and her brothers have inspired her to be warmer, more understanding, more accepting of her children's bids for attention and comfort. Whatever hurts or injuries she suffered in childhood would be made irrelevant by the force of her love, a mother's love, and by her commitment to rear them more ably than she herself had been raised.

———

In every nursery there are ghosts," child psychoanalyst Selma Fraiberg wrote. In every mother's life, we hear the strains of the relationship we had with our own mothers, we catch its resonance as it ebbs and flows into and out of the ones we are creating with our own children. Some of us hesitate, unsure of what value reflecting on the past might hold for our children and for ourselves. Some of us, like Gloria, refuse to acknowledge the past because we consider nothing insurmountable in the face of personal resolve. What I have observed many times is that telling a mother's story does not harm a child or a relationship. Instead, what is damaging is a mother's refusal to acknowledge this tie, that it is powerful, and that it is often evident in a wholly new way once we become mothers ourselves.

———

Margaret could not bring herself to tell her children about her own childhood, believing it too harsh and incomprehensible. To tell them about it felt like an indictment of her parents. Their sending her away was an act she thought would not seem loving, but heartless and cruel. Margaret never found a way to relieve her childhood burden of living with an absence that could not be acknowledged, a longing that could not be expressed. Day in and day out, she and her children lived Lucky's empty good fortune, an intimate, unspoken tale that passed from mother to child, its theme the belief that children can grow up just fine without love.

———

This pattern of recurrence, the retelling of our childhood stories in our relationship to our children is revealed not only in the closely observed hours of psychoanalytic theorists, but in some very elegant and groundbreaking research conducted by developmental psychologist Mary Main. Main is an attachment theorist who had been a student of Mary Ainsworth, herself a student of the originator of attachment theory, the British psychoanalyst John Bowlby. Bowlby developed his theory of the nature and purpose of the tie between mother and infant during the 1950s and '60s. Twenty years earlier as a newly trained child psychiatrist in England, Bowlby had been deeply troubled by the negative consequences of early and protracted separations between mothers and babies. Such separations occurred routinely in hospitals at the time. Over the next thirty years he refined and tested his ideas, arriving at a model that is primarily concerned with identifying the factors that allow children to tolerate the stress of separations from their mothers.

As used by attachment theorists, the term attachment does not refer to an affective or social bond. It refers instead to a particular aspect of the parent-child relationship, the child's faith that the parents will protect him from physical and psychological harm. According to the theory, this faith is what allows a child to move away from the immediate protective presence of the parent to explore the world around him. It serves as the child's "secure base."

Through the thousands of interactions with the parent from infancy onward, every child acquires a set of expectations regarding the regularity, reliability and sensitivity of the parent's care. She develops a mental representation of the parent as caregiver and of the history of that parent's responsiveness to her. This mental representation is what attachment theorists call the "internal working model." It consists not only of the child's image of the parent, but also the child's image of himself as a partner in the relationship. If, for example, a mother is regularly responsive to her child at times of stress, attending to her need for comfort and support, the child's working model will most likely represent the mother as sensitive, reliable and helpful, and the child herself as someone deserving of the mother's help and attention.

Most of the research on attachment theory originally focused on describing the nature of the child's working model. In the mid-1980s, however, Main began to study the internal working models of parents. Just as Freud was convinced that listening to a patient's free associations was the inroad to the unconscious, Main was convinced that listening to how a parent spoke about their childhood would reveal the character of her internal working model. Main's goal was to establish links between a parent's memories, or what are known in attachment theory as "mental representations," and the kind of attachment the parent's child developed to him or her.

To do this, parents were asked to select five adjectives to describe their mothers and five to describe their fathers, and then to explain why these particular adjectives came to mind; to describe what they did when upset as a child; whether they felt their parents had been rejecting, and if so, what they thought about that experience now; whether their relationship with their parents had undergone change since childhood; and how their childhood experiences had shaped the person they had become. When the parents' answers were analyzed using a method from psycholinguistics known as discourse analysis, three patterns of parental attachment were revealed, which Main labeled: "dismissive," "preoccupied" and "autonomous."

Mothers dismissive of attachment had difficulty reflecting on the history of their relationship to their parents, frequently saying that they did not remember their childhoods. They spoke only vaguely at first or in idealizing terms about their mothers and fathers. But when pressed for details by the interviewer, these mothers eventually described harsh and traumatic childhood memories. One parent described her mother as "nice," but when she was asked to elaborate on this quality, she could not. As the interview progressed, it became clear that her mother drank a good deal and was often angry and hostile toward her. This mother, like many other "dismissive" parents, regarded the harsh treatment from their parents as promoting strength of character, and denied any enduring negative consequences to their parents' actions.

"Preoccupied" mothers spoke about their parents with obvious unresolved feelings of disappointment, hurt and anger. As adults, these mothers remained intent upon pleasing their parents and gaining their approval. Their memories were confused and often incoherently articulated. The intensity of their feeling about their parents disrupted their train of thought and created a jumbled, disconnected set of impressions and feelings. Mothers preoccupied with their childhood relationships seemed not to have gained much distance or perspective on their parents, but remained embroiled in their childhood struggle for attention and recognition.

In contrast to these mothers, an "autonomous" mother spoke of the relationships to her parents with obvious comfort and perspective, giving a balanced, realistic picture of childhood. The descriptions revealed insight into both the negative and positive aspects of these relationships, and an ability to reflect on the conflicts and disappointments with parents with compassion and forgiveness. The autonomous mothers did not have childhoods that were freer of family conflicts and stress than the childhoods of the dismissive or preoccupied mothers, and their parents did not appear to be more psychologically well balanced. What set the autonomous mothers apart was their having found ways to reflect constructively on the relationship to their parents. Main described one such mother in this way, "One mother who had been strongly rejected by her family laughed at our initial query regarding the nature of her early relationships and asked, 'How many hours do you have? Okay, well, to start with, my mother was not cheerful, and I can tell you right now, the reason was that she was overworked.'"

A mother's reflection and acceptance of her childhood not only enhanced her sense of well-being, but also had a clear bearing on the kind of attachment relationship her child established with her. Autonomous mothers had children who were securely attached to them both as one-year-olds and as six-year-olds. Whereas, three-quarters of the children of "dismissive" mothers were similarly dismissive of their relationship to her. They acted as though their mother's comings and goings did not affect them at all. They were polite, but aloof and indifferent to her. Children of preoccupied mothers, in a manner that corresponded to their mother's relationship to her own parents, tended to vacillate between strong avoidance of her and an equally intense desire to be physically close following separation. They seemed depressed or confused and had difficulty expressing emotions in a clear and direct fashion. As six-year-olds, they reacted to separation from her by becoming physically aggressive, clingy or excessively and inappropriately solicitous, adopting a caretaking role toward her.

————

The importance of Mary Main's findings are extraordinary and twofold. First, they demonstrate the continuity of the past in the present. Second, and not to be slighted, is her finding that the past is not necessarily re-created unaltered in our present relationships with our children. Main's work shows that mothers who had troubled childhood relationships with their parents could nonetheless form secure bonds with their own children if they had achieved an understanding and emotional acceptance of their parents. This second, and perhaps more significant, finding is well supported in subsequent work by other attachment theorists, most notably that of Peter Fonagy and his colleagues.

Unfortunately, I think the second point is too often drowned out by the first. It seems we are still stuck with the old idea that we are destined to repeat the past. After all these years I understand that Margaret was trying to tell me this is what happened to her. Her past had become her destiny as a mother. I think she wanted me to know she had tried her best to be a good mother, asking that I not judge her too harshly. Maybe she secretly hoped I would use what she had told me to comfort her daughter.

———

To reveal ourselves in a compromised light, not as women, but as mothers, is a struggle for many of us. The categories "good" and "bad" so easily come to mind as we try to understand other mothers and to understand ourselves as mothers. For instance, if you are anything like me, you will not have been reading Main's research findings with detachment, responding to them purely as information. You will have been reading with a suppressed question. You will probably have been asking, "Which kind of mother am I? 'Good' or 'bad'?"

Most of us inherit the expectation that mothers are to be models of perfection from our mothers who, in their need to be "good" mothers themselves, offered few clues about their histories or struggles to fulfill this burdensome image of motherhood. Those few hints that slipped out from the busy activity of their mothering, like the lace trim on a slip, were discreetly drawn up and out of view. For a few moments, Margaret let her slip show, telling me bits of the story she had long hidden from her children and from herself. I wish she had spoken to my friend Ellen as she had spoken to me, but I know she never did.

My friend Gloria and I talked again a few days after she called me. The conversation was more awkward than I would like to admit. I could sense that she feared that I

was judging her, and I kept tripping over my wish to re-
assure her that what happened with her son was a once in
a lifetime occurrence. But Gloria knew better. Seeing
Joe's hurt expression had shaken her, and the thought that
she had probably hurt her mother in exactly the same way,
many times over the years, popped into her head for the
first time. She hadn't really put her feelings about her
mother to rest, just fooled herself into believing she could
banish them from her life as a mother. Musing aloud,
Gloria thought she had to avoid acknowledging her
mother as fragile and vulnerable because having a mother
who couldn't take care of herself was just too overwhelming. There was a long pause, and Gloria said softly, "Until my outburst, I wasn't aware of how much I have
wanted Joe to be tough because my mother was not. I let
myself forget that he is just a little boy. That it's human
to be soft, to be vulnerable. I talked with him last night.
It was just a few minutes, and he only grunted at me. But
we both felt better."

——

Since that conversation with Gloria, I have wondered if in
those repetitions from our past there isn't a distinct maternal desire at work. At a time when our identities are
undergoing enormous change, we find shelter in the familiar. Nestled in my anxious protective measures as a
new mother was a fantasy that if I just kept trying it my
mother's way I would feel I was being a good mother. But
more important, by doing it my mother's way, I wouldn't
have to figure out what being "a good mother" meant to

me. I could avoid the work of discovering the kind of mother *my* children needed me to be. I see this same desire for a shortcut to feeling like a good mother in Gloria's resolution, too.

I realize it isn't always easy to approach motherhood as a "work in progress." Doing so is contrary to the popular notion that finding an answer to a question quickly and effortlessly means that you are really good, really smart, really capable. This is true even when it comes to a question as big as what kind of mother do you want to be. Living through those minutes, days and sometimes months of uncertainty is necessary to arrive at an answer. It's also hard at times. But I am certain you will be glad if you do, listening to the past in the present, open and unafraid.

A CHILD IS CRYING

What Our Children's Distress
Can Tell Us

On a warm summer evening a few years ago, I was out in front of the house pulling weeds. Bent over the brick walkway, I heard laughter at the far end of the street. I looked up to see our next-door neighbor Kevin's car stopped in front of the house on the corner. The couple that lives there, Liz and Mark, seemed to be enjoying a joke with Kevin. After a few minutes, Mark, who is very tall and lanky, straightened himself up and lightly and affectionately tapped the roof of the car. Kevin continued to drive down the street, but slowly, stopping to chat briefly with whoever happened to be out. Watching the leisurely pace of this drive, I was pretty sure he was announcing the arrival of the new baby. His wife Laura had been a week past her due date, and she and two-year-old Michael, an effervescent little dynamo, were nowhere to be seen. Ordinarily on such a nice night Mikey would have been charging around the yard, beeping, tooting and vrooming, vehicles being his passion, and it was unusually quiet next door.

When Kevin pulled into his driveway, he got out of the car and ambled over. He was grinning from ear to ear, and before I could ask whether the baby was a boy or a girl, he gleefully announced, "No dimples!" I laughed thinking immediately of Michael's charming, dimpled face, an exact replica of Laura's. "No dimples," he repeated with satisfaction, "and she has my chin!" he added for emphasis. I understood Kevin's shorthand perfectly. That's because most everyone says that my children look like me, and that they look like each other.

For many years whenever anyone commented about Emily and Rachel's resemblance to me, I would demur, pointing out the ways the girls also looked like their father. I would point to the roundness of Emily's eyes and the tilt at the end of her nose; to Rachel's slender face and the red highlights in her hair. But both girls have dark straight hair and dark eyes, while people mistakenly assume their father is Scandinavian because he is blond and blue-eyed. My efforts to right the balance in people's perception thus usually fall on deaf ears and are met with expressions of disbelief. ("You've got to be kidding!" "You aren't blind are you?") Yet I keep trying to find ways of interjecting that he is in fact in their genetic mix. I persist out of a sense of loyalty to my husband; I want him to get some credit, too. I also persist because it eases my conscience about how much pleasure I can feel about this affirmation, even this superficial one, that they belong to me, and that we belong together.

My biologist friend Henry says ethologists look upon this enjoyment as a natural evolution-determined parental response, a safeguard against parents abandoning their young. Genetic similarities between parent and child are believed to pave the way for a parent to be sensitively and accurately attuned to subtle fluctuations in a baby's state of being. It seems that to see aspects of ourselves reflected in our children heightens our investment in caring for them. He shares with me fascinating examples of this mechanism, known simply as "recognition," describing it as an aspect of the attachment between parent and child. He tells me that mother sheep and mother goats routinely reject any newborn that is not theirs, but if an orphaned lamb or kid is bathed with a prospective adoptive mother's milk, she no longer rejects it, but accepts it as hers. He describes strategies which have evolved in certain penguins to ensure babies are reunited with their mother following separation, and he tells me about mother free-tail bats, who, with nearly 100 percent accuracy, pick out their own tiny infant from among three thousand others, relying on their baby's distinctive smell and vocalizations. He reminds me that human mothers similarly learn to identify their own newborn's cry and begin to distinguish their cries of fatigue and of hunger.

Henry wants me to believe that nature always works

wisely and well. He wants to convince me that the same mechanisms that have evolved in response to a species' need for survival, work well for me, an individual human mother, too. But, I am skeptical. It is not that I dismiss the ideas from evolutionary biology as irrelevant to me. I accept that as biological creatures we are shaped by the imperatives "to survive to reproductive age, to reproduce and to rear offspring until they reach reproductive age." It is just that parents in our industrialized society with its lengthy period of childhood dependence not only have a reproductive investment in their offspring, but a psychological one, as well. I doubt, for example, that the plain brown sparrows I watch through my kitchen window ever feel anything like I feel as I glimpse my youthful athleticism in my child streaking down a soccer field for a goal, or childhood curiosity about the physical world as she examines and categorizes rocks. I'm pretty sure my fellow mothers in the creature world don't feel pride and pleasure over things like this. And I am even more certain that they are not tempted to coax their offspring, as I know I can be tempted, into becoming a particular kind of person for the sake of their own pleasure, fulfillment and comfort. This, I suspect, exists as a uniquely human possibility.

———

My lunchtime conversations with Henry got me to think more seriously about recognition, and how much more complexly it works for us as human mothers. It seems to me there is an aspect of human recognition that comes closer in meaning to "affinity" or "compatibility." Usually when we talk about feeling compatible with another person, we are describing relationships with friends and partners, and not our relationships with our children. Yet, we can all probably think of families where children fit, or don't fit well, with their parents. Parents who are nature lovers and avid campers have a quiet bookish child who hates to sweat. Taciturn, socially withdrawn parents end up with a very talkative, sociable child who knows everyone she meets walking in town. Professional parents are estranged when their children choose to become carpenters and stone masons and choose not to write books. But even before these kinds of divergences of interest and expectation become apparent, there is another kind of divergence that can exist between parents and children. I am thinking here of differences in what developmental psychologists call temperament or behavioral style. Here are some examples:

Nancy is a high-energy person who plays and works hard. But her first baby was quiet and slow and is not especially adaptable in new situations. She couldn't get him to move fast enough to keep up with her and her usual habits. Everything had to be done slowly, methodically, without variation, without skipping any steps. He seemed to retreat from stimulation. Lights, talking and noises of all kinds bothered him. He'd shut his eyes, his little body would tense up and then he would cry for a very long time. Nancy couldn't take him anywhere and that drove her crazy.

"I constantly feel the need to protect Kate from the

baby," Janet told me. "Hannah is so much more physical than Kate. And me too, I guess. I used to think I was lucky to have girls. I assumed I wouldn't be dealing with all that raw physical energy that boys seem to have, and that all my friends with boys talk about. But Hannah is like a bulldozer, literally and figuratively. She's broad and low to the ground, and she is very strong. Kate and I will be working on a project and Hannah, fresh from her afternoon nap, will come barreling into the room. I know she just wants to be part of what we're doing, but I feel like she is always destroying our peace and quiet."

Nancy and Janet are typical mothers. They get frustrated and angry with their children who are by nature temperamentally different from themselves. They have probably said some things to their children that in hindsight they would have preferred not to have said, been less patient, less tolerant, less understanding than they would have like to have been, but I know them to be loving mothers, completely devoted to their children. They often feel that they are terrible mothers when they are really good mothers, good mothers trying their best to cope with a child whose disposition is different from theirs. They each have a child whose characteristic ways of relating, reacting and doing things in the world feel unfamiliar and different from their own.

Temperamental matches such as these can be one of the toughest challenges a mother can face. It is hard work living with a child with whom you feel a basic incompatibility. It isn't hard all the time, or always hard in the same way at every phase of a child's development. But being in such a relationship requires considerable energy, self-awareness and flexibility. When you are in such a relationship you can, without intending or sometimes even noticing it, turn away from him or her, not physically, but in terms of the quality of the attention you give to them, and the kind of responsiveness to their needs you offer. This happens more easily in our relationships with these children because we do not instinctively and automatically understand their reactions. The things that bring them contentment and pleasure do not affect us in the same way. And it can be especially difficult to hear their distress because the aspects of the environment that disturb them, do not naturally stress us. We have to work harder to imagine the world from their point of view. We have to work to get past our reactions to their differences. In this way, such temperamental dissimilarities between mother and child can become impediments to attentive love.

Until the late 1960s, psychological theories did not look upon the mother-child relationship as a two-way street. People believed babies were all about the same, and so any differences in behavior and development between them were thought to follow directly from differences in the care they received from their mothers. For example, if a baby cried a lot and was hard to soothe, the common wisdom was that the mother was anxious and communicating her anxiety to the baby. The baby was crying purely in response to her distress. The notion that some babies are by nature more difficult to calm was not part of the generally accepted understanding of what babies are supposed to be like and how they were supposed to behave.

Experienced mothers knew even then, of course, that every baby had his or her distinctive way of being in the world. They understood that babies had natural predispositions that influenced how easy or difficult it was to care for them. From their own experience, they could see, for instance, that their babies developed sleeping habits at different rates and in different patterns. A mother might observe that one of her children loved to be cuddled and to be sung to before falling asleep, and she slept through the night at eight weeks. Another of her babies preferred being left on a hard surface like a bedroom rug before drifting off in a dark, noiseless room, and woke himself up several times every night until he was almost a year. Yet another never slept during the day more than twenty minutes at a stretch, and was always cheerful, active and happy. These were differences that seemed to have little to do with what a mother did or didn't do. They were differences in the babies themselves.

During the 1960s and 1970s, the research of child psychiatrists Alexander Thomas and Stella Chess began to bridge the gap between the prevailing outlook on babies and the knowledge of experienced mothers. Based on observations of thousands of infants, they found that there are differences in babies' styles of interacting with the world that are apparent from a few months of age. They introduced the term "temperament" to describe such differences.

Temperament refers to "the distinct, yet normal, behavioral patterns that babies bring to various situations." It is not the same as personality; it is not intelligence, or determined by intelligence. Nor is it a reflection of a baby's general emotional and behavioral adjustment. It is the baby's stylistic approach to the world, and "it affects how they experience and respond to a multitude of environments." A baby's temperament is defined by nine characteristics:

Activity level. Some babies are physically more active, some are less active.

Regularity. Babies differ in their biological rhythms, eating, sleeping and eliminating in a regular or irregular way.

Approach or withdrawal. Babies differ in their characteristic reaction to a new situation. Babies greet new situations more or less positively.

Adaptability to change in routine. Babies respond differently to change over an extended time.

Sensitivity. Level of sensory threshold. Variations in how babies react to bright light, noise, confusion, being wet, wearing clothes with different textures. Some babies are bothered more by these experiences than others.

Positive or negative mood. Characteristic mood.

Intensity of response. Level of energy expended.

Persistence and attention span. Variation in babies' ability to continue an activity in the face of difficulty or to resume it after interruption.

Distractibility. Refers to babies' degree of concentration. Some babies concentrate without distraction, others do not.

Babies with positive mood, for instance, "smile often and spontaneously, laugh a lot, and are friendly with most people." Babies whose predominant mood state is negative "react with unpleasant, unfriendly responses; they are fussy, complaining, and less amiable around other people." Intensity, as another example, "refers to the amount of energy in the child's response, regardless of whether it is positive and happy or negative and fussy. An intense child both laughs and cries loudly. A milder child just smiles and whimpers.

Thomas and Chess were originally interested in identifying the temperament features that were associated with "difficult to manage" infants, believing these children were at a greater risk for problems in development than babies that were less demanding to care for. They defined "difficult" babies as timid in their initial reactions, slow to adapt, high in intensity, predominantly negative in mood and irregular. "Easy" babies, by contrast, were defined as pleasant, flexible, not too intense and fairly predictable. After thirty years of temperament studies by various investigators, we know that almost half of the children studied have "easy" temperaments, about 40 percent of children have mixtures of traits, and the remaining 10 percent have "difficult" temperaments. It is also clear that temperament is not purely an expression of a child's genes, but is also influenced by environmental factors.

Harvard developmental psychologist Jerome Kagan has studied a temperament dimension he has called "inhibited versus uninhibited to the unfamiliar." His research of the last twenty years indicates that approximately 10 to 15 percent of Caucasian infants and children react to unfamiliar people, settings and challenges with fearfulness and timidity. These children respond very predictably to novelty by becoming distressed and anxious. As infants they cry intensely and show a great deal of motor activity; as two-year-olds they are extremely shy with strangers and timid in new situations. Although some "inhibited" children become less reactive to novelty over the course of their development, the majority of these children retain their characteristic response to new situations until they are about eight years old. Uninhibited children, by contrast, are sociable and show spontaneous and positive emotional expression in their reaction to unfamiliar people and circumstances. Kagan estimates that approximately 15 percent of Caucasian children are "uninhibited."

Very interestingly, the two behavioral responses, "inhibited" and "uninhibited" to novelty, appear to be associated with distinctive physiological patterns, which in turn implicate different sites and/or mechanisms of brain activity. These physiological correlates suggest "differential thresholds in the limbic system to novel and challenging events." Kagan stresses the importance of not assuming that environmental factors do not play a role in temperament. He points out that associations between physiological profiles and behavioral ones do not justify the conclusion that temperament is purely genetically determined. He and colleague Nancy Snidman state, "We suggest only that some infants are born with a physiology that biases them to develop one rather than another behavioral surface, given certain environments."

————

The most recent temperament research focuses directly on the question of how a baby's temperament interacts with that of the mother. In general, when there is a close match between the temperaments of baby and mother, mothers readily demonstrate sensitivity and responsiveness to their children's communication of emotion; as the temperament difference widens, it becomes more difficult for mothers to be sensitive and responsive. However, it is when a mother's temperament differs from her child's that her sensitivity and responsiveness are especially important. Developmental psychologists have found that differences in maternal sensitivity are associated with different developmental outcomes in children.

For example, Ruth Feldman and her colleagues report that infants whose mothers are sensitively responsive to their feelings are more likely when they become toddlers to show positive behaviors such as self-control. In this research, a toddler child demonstrated self-control by complying with a mother's requests and by delaying action when asked to. Not surprisingly, it was much easier for mothers whose babies are of easygoing temperaments to be sensitive and responsive. These were the mothers whose babies were most likely as toddlers to show self-control. More interesting though was the finding that temperamentally demanding babies who demonstrated comparable self-control at age two had mothers who had learned to accommodate their difficult temperaments. The mothers of these children resisted the temptation to disengage from interactions, to take over their interactions, or to give in to the child's negativity with negativity of her own.

Sometimes when a mother tries to respect her child's particular temperamental characteristics she encounters the negative judgment of others. A mother of a highly sensitive child, a child who cries out as though in pain because his socks rumple at the end of his sneakers, because his toast is too crunchy, and because his sheets don't smell "regular," is likely to question herself a good deal, and vacillate between trying to respect this temperamental trait and trying to get her child not to make such a big deal out of everything. In a society that esteems cheerfulness in girls and ruggedness in boys, her child is seen as "finicky," "complaining" and "whiney." And everyone assumes that she has created this persnickety creature because she has been too indulgent, too protective, giving into his sensitivities far too often. Holding onto a sense that you are being a good mother by resisting these judgments is important to your sense of well-being and confidence as a mother.

———

Sometimes I work with a mother who says she finds the notion of temperamental match and mismatch helpful in dealing with her difficult child, yet she continues to doubt that she is being a good and loving mother. After enough discussion, we usually discover deep down she believes that a mother's love should be neutral, never preferential. Much like Switzerland during times of war, she feels she can't declare any feeling of affinity or lack of compatibility when it comes to her children. In our culture, acknowledging preferences for certain qualities feels perilously close to declaring you love one child "best." We have a common vision that in a good mother's heart, everyone is the same. Good mothers do not notice, admit or act on difference. Good mothers are supposed to feel exactly the same about every child, no matter how different from her and irrespective of the child's native characteristics. This notion of a mother's love as nonspecific and impersonal frequently intimidates mothers into acting as though their children are all the same when they are not. Rather than supporting a sense of closeness between mother and child, it denies how real children and real mothers feel about one another in a way that can interfere with a robust and honest basis for love.

———

I remember a therapy hour with eleven-year-old David and his mother Lisa. Lisa and David's father had never been married and neither David nor his brother Sam had ever known their father. Lisa wanted some guidance as she and David explored his request that he be allowed to contact his father. I could feel the estrangement widen between David and Lisa during a therapy session when David asked his mother to tell him what she loved about him. After a lot of thought, Lisa gave an answer that I could see she felt proud of. It was an answer that stayed in the bounds of our generally accepted image of a mother's love. This meant that it could not be an answer that acknowledged the idiosyncratic, unique, particular characteristics of her child, the qualities that made David, David, and not his brother Sam. In keeping with the principle that a mother's love should be neutral Lisa said, "I love you because you are my first-born son."

David's reaction to his mother's answer was to be hurt and angry. He rattled off a list of things Lisa could have said to satisfy him, to make it clear that she knew him as a specific person with specific and particular attributes. When she could not, he felt that she mustn't love him because she couldn't think of anything about his interests, his personality, his assets, even his faults. Lisa could not understand why he felt the way he did.

———

It probably would not have occurred to me that love and temperament have much to do with one another, if it weren't for Emily and Rachel. I remember that as a student I had to write a comprehensive examination paper on the subject of infant temperament. I cut up a copy of Thomas and Chess's temperament questionnaire and made a set of flashcards by pasting each individual behavior to the blank side of a three-by-five-inch index card. On the opposite side, I neatly wrote the name of one of the nine factors it was related to. When my set was complete, I sat down in the little puddle of late autumn sunshine near my bed. I studied the cards one at a time, trying to decide whether "at bathtime, kicks, splashes and dives under water so energetically, there's a lake on the bathroom floor every night" went into, "high intensity"? or "high activity"? As I drilled myself, reading, debating, trying to gain speed and certainty with each pass, I remember daydreaming about the qualities I would want a baby of mine to have. He or she would be not too intense, spontaneous and expressive, easily adaptable to change, cuddly. I also remember thinking with the naïveté of a woman not yet a mother, that it wouldn't matter, I would be the same mother to my children no matter what "kind" of child I had.

Ten years later, I did have my easy baby. With Emily I was not pressed to love a child who reacts to the world in vastly different ways than I do. Instead, I have known comfort akin to being with an old friend, a familiar self. She was a dream baby, eating and sleeping regularly, easy and quick to soothe, quiet and eminently portable. As she got older, she continued to be an accommodating child with a sweet, happy disposition. My husband and I watched her amiable spirit unfold with great joy, her temperament well matched to ours. We were a textbook example of felicitous "goodness of fit."

From time to time as she got older, I would wonder if

I wasn't just imagining our perfect compatibility, simply enlarging and exaggerating our similarities, each an embellishment upon the conviction that we fit together perfectly. I wondered if I was overlooking our differences, selectively discarding all that contradicted this view. But I didn't really sense any danger then in continuing in this way, and we went along happily for seven years enjoying an easy and comfortable companionship.

Then we had Rachel. My fairy godmother must have decided I could handle a challenge because she sent me a baby that was not so easy as the first, not outright difficult according to the Thomas and Chess criteria, but one that had different requirements than her sister. As a baby, Rachel was not the easy, regular baby Emily had been. High on sensitivity. Low on distractibility. Low on regularity. Low on adaptability. What we all remember was that she cried a lot. My husband and I walked for hours on end, making circle after circle through the downstairs rooms—living room, hallway, family room, kitchen, dining room, living room, hallway, family room, over and over, and still she cried. She was one of those babies who was not easily distracted from her distress. And she was not a good sleeper, whereas Emily slept through the night early and took a nap every day until she went to kindergarten.

Rachel stood and talked and walked early, and she has grown into an active little girl with a very energetic and inquiring mind. She is, as her day-care mom Cheri says, "always trying to figure something out." Indeed, Rachel's desire to know about things is insatiable. She often pummels me with questions I cannot answer. She asks how to make water run uphill with the same ease as it runs downhill. (We consult her engineer grandfather about this.) She pounces on a microscopic speck of sand and demands to know whether she has found mica. Sadly for Rachel, I can think only of Micah, Lucus McCain's friend in the television show *The Rifleman*. Some days I think she needs an encyclopedia not a mother, or maybe a mother whose knowledge is encyclopedic. I sigh realizing how many times every day she must feel I fail her.

Rachel asks a lot about God, too. How can God have existed before "he or she" had a mother? If God loves us, then why is "he or she" keeping Aunt Laurie in heaven with her since she could not possibly love her more than we do? I feel stymied in the face of these questions, in the face of Rachel's wish for certain and immutable categories, and her drive to make the world logical, consistent and completely knowable when it is not. "This is why I don't want to be in life," she once lamented to me. My poor Rachel. Unlike her sister, unlike me, the disorderly, enigmatic aspects of human existence baffle and frustrate her. I know she feels this difference. And I am certain it is sometimes a difference that makes her feel more alone. More alone and, I fear, less loved.

One evening the girls and I were playing together in Rachel's bedroom when seemingly out of the blue Rachel said to me, "You *let* Emily be born first!" Here was the irrefutable evidence that I love her less than her sister. I was dumbfounded, and I looked helplessly at this child who seems almost by virtue of her constitution to reject the idea that things happen by chance. She stood erect, wide-eyed, her entire body taut as she rid herself of this accusation. I was stunned by the weight of Rachel's conclusion. I knew this was not merely a declaration of envy, or a four-year-old's attempt at manipulation. It was too heartfelt and anguished. My friend Annie believes her younger child, arriving five years after her first, felt from the very beginning that she was breaking into a "very settled" family. A family that felt complete without her. This was what Rachel felt, shut out from the assurance of my love for her, not by accident, but by design.

I asked myself in how many different ways had she tried to get through to me. How many times had I not listened well enough to her distress, brushing it aside as her excessive sensitivity, her tendency to make a mountain out of a molehill, and bullied her into squashing her natural reactions because "in the long run" it would be better for her? Perhaps I had taken refuge in my easier relationship with Emily more than I even knew. Undone, I could only hold her, crumbled in a little heap and sobbing in my arms, letting the rush of reassurance that I love her as much as her sister subside, unspoken.

I think about that evening with Rachel, and I am grateful for her tenacious spirit, and grateful that she did not give up on me. I had wanted to persuade her that she was mistaken, to defend myself, and to declare that I love her no less tenderly or abundantly than I love her sister.

Only I knew Rachel was speaking a hard truth, and about a hurt that could not be eased with a quick hug and a few reassuring words. She was telling me about attentive love, but at a time when I didn't have a name for the love she was telling me she needed. She was describing love that moves a mother to *unsettle* herself and become, if just for a while, someone other than who she is natively and naturally. She does this so she might love her children not as she is inclined, but as they are meant and need to be. I won't pretend I don't struggle still with this demanding aspect of love in my day-to-day life as a mother. But even if I don't get it right every time, I've learned that it is important to keep trying. What good, after all, is my love if it comes in a form that does not suit who Rachel is and what she needs?

————

So, I had a child like me (or so it seemed), one not much like me (and so this seemed, too), sisters who look alike, yet who are distinct in their reactions and relationships to the world, and to me. I no longer accept as an enduring truth the simple symmetry that Emily is like me and Rachel is not. I see Emily, the child I thought I knew so well, exploring new facets of herself, facets we do not share, less wary, it seems to me, that doing so carries the risk of losing her mother's love and approval. I have come to see that our sameness, however innocent, comfortable and accurate in its origins can become an illusion, one that constrains the fullness of who she is. And I've found sources of compatibility with Rachel that Emily and I don't share. Like me, Rachel is precise, and can keep track of people, places and events. We are planners; and we are methodical in the execution of whatever we plan. Long after everyone else gives up, we are carefully sorting through the thousand pieces of our latest jigsaw puzzle, matching color and texture until each piece is examined and then assigned its place.

As I appreciate and accept that my children are much more complex than the simple dichotomy, like me–not like me, they too seem to grow in their appreciation of each other. Rachel's exuberance infects us all, but it has meant the most to her sister. Emily looks for Rachel after school to chase and horse around with, glad for the chance to be wild and silly and loud. Rachel likes to snuggle next to Emily, soaking in her peacefulness. Often Rachel asks to listen to a CD on her sister's Discman. They lie on their stomachs on Emily's bedroom floor, the CD player between them. Each wears headphones, their heads bobbing in unison to the songs only they can hear. A concert just for them.

Rachel confessed not long ago that she worries a lot about my dying. She says she doesn't know who will understand the way she feels about things, or who will understand about her feelings at all if I am suddenly gone. I think she was asking who will interpret her "high sensitivity" and "low distractibility" to the rest of the world. In a funny way that maybe only mothers can understand, I took her statement as confirmation that I've been doing a better job at being her mom. I've gotten clearer that I can and need to be a different mother with each of my daughters and that doing so isn't about loving one of them more than the other. I've given up the idea that a mother's love is generic, that one size should fit all. Thinking about attentive love has helped me to redirect my energy as a mother, away from ignoring or gritting my teeth in the face of my children's differences with me, toward cultivating a willingness to listen for their particular expressions of the person each of them is, even if they are expressions unlike my own.

————

Rachel is still intense; she is still sensitive. She is the member of the family who laughs the loudest and the hardest and is the first to get a joke and tell one. When she cries, she cries very loud and very long. I don't try to get her to stop any more, well, at least, most of the time I don't. We all know when Rachel is unhappy. And we try our best to let her be unhappy for as long as she needs to be, having learned that just as when she was a baby, distraction doesn't work, and it probably never will. She likes company when she is crying and so I try my best to push aside the inner voice that says I don't have time for this, that she is going on far too long, that it really shouldn't be that big deal. I don't always pull it off, but always isn't necessary. Most of the time is what is possible. In fact, most of the time is pretty perfect.

HEARING THE UNSPOKEN

Understanding Silence as Expression

A lot of people have the idea that therapists are good talk-ers, and that is one reason they become therapists. This is probably true for many of the therapists I know. They are individuals who have a natural facility with speech, for whom verbal expression comes swiftly and gracefully. Many of my colleagues paint eloquent and moving pic-tures whenever they speak, pictures that go right to the heart of any matter. I, on the other hand, am really not much of a talker. I speak with pauses and hesitation, to the outside observer, as though I am searching for just the right word. When truthfully what I am doing is search-ing for any word. I know it might be hard to believe, but conversing, letting my thoughts come out freely, is harder for me than most.

As you can imagine this was a problem for an aspiring therapist. At the beginning of my training, I had to remind myself very deliberately that telling another person what I thought about him or her was considered helpful, not simply a rude intrusion into their private thoughts and feelings. A therapy teacher of mine once insisted, the frustration in his voice rising, "You must *tell* your patient what you understand about her. That is, after all, why she is coming to see you. You *must* tell her what you just told me." Intellectually, I understood how I was supposed to be relating to my patient. I understood that it isn't enough to just say "um" and "tell me more," but when I tried, I kept bumping up against a feeling that I was doing something wrong, violating a principle I didn't even know I possessed about how to treat others. I couldn't explain either to myself or to him why I felt that way. And because I couldn't, I looked at myself (and so did he) as afflicted by a strange and unusual psychological impairment, one that would prevent me from ever being a therapist. Talking allows the relationship between therapist and patient to develop, and it is how a therapist communicates her understanding and support. It was pretty clear I couldn't really be a therapist unless I overcame this reticence.

Although at the time I didn't know what my discomfort was about, I did know that what I liked about doing therapy was not the talking, but the listening. I am sure this is why I loved and still love to do therapy with young children, because when children are three or five or eight years old, they don't usually talk much in therapy, they play instead. They play out their feelings about themselves and the important people in their lives. They play out endlessly fascinating stories that are full of profound and sometimes heartbreaking feelings. Over the years, my young patients have cast me in a thousand roles: a pirate stranded on a desert island, a mother who forgets to take her baby with her when she goes on trips, a weary subject of an imperious and mercurial king, and I've been animals of all sorts, mostly cats, I would say. On other occasions, I am merely a witness to emotional dramas played out with dolls in the dollhouse or puppets that pop out from under a desk or from behind a chair. When the arcade game Pac-Man was popular, I spent many hours being pursued by a munching eight-year-old up and down and across the markings of a basketball court.

Children play like this, not automatically and immediately, but after they come to trust that the therapy office and the relationship they have with me are reliable, safe and unchanging. They must find the same toys, in the same places, every time they come. They must find the same things on the walls and on the desk. We must start at the same time, and end at the same time, when the minute hand of the clock is on the ten. And if I do my job right, they will let me know an awful lot about the scary and painful events that have happened to them and the thoughts and feelings that go along with them.

I think of my patient Michelle, aged four. She divided her time between two activities, making paper collages of people's faces that buckled from the weight of the glue and locking up the father doll and mother doll into the dollhouse, and then throwing the key away. Week after week she alternated between these two activities, expressions of her frustration that her parents were more involved with their drinking than they were with her. They were never where she wanted and needed them to be in real life, but in the fantasy that she created in her therapy, she was in charge of their comings and goings. And when she was in charge, she could keep her feelings of sadness and loneliness from overtaking her.

There are times when children convey their feelings in a way that can be hard for a therapist to listen to. Working with nine-year-old Sean was like that for me. Sean's mother died very suddenly from a brain tumor when he was eight. In each session he managed to give me a news report about children who had been violently injured. I'd hear about car accidents, explosions, fires and falls from windows. He knew every grim and gory detail and recounted them all, often using toy cars and trucks to demonstrate the catastrophes as he imagined them, with sounds of the crashing cars, the voices of the helpless children, and with the chronic and glaring absence of helpful, concerned or responsible adults. This was how he let me know that his mother's early death had left him feeling unbearably vulnerable in a world that now felt dangerous and vacant of love and protection. Finding the words to describe these feelings was impossible, so he acted them out for me instead.

For Michelle and Sean playing like this was therapeutic.

It allowed them both to express and master difficult and painful feelings and experiences. It isn't necessary however for children to be in therapy for them to use play in the same way, as a way to master new situations and the feelings that those situations evoke. Not long ago Rachel and a friend from school were playing upstairs in her bedroom. As I approached Rachel's room to see how they were doing, I heard Amanda singing and Rachel spelling. I knocked and asked what they were doing. They happily shouted back that they were playing school. "School?" I said. "Yes! School," they replied, then added, "It's a FREE school." Surprised and intrigued, I let my curiosity take over and I leaned my head into the room and said, "What do you mean free? You mean you don't have to pay to go to school here?" Grinning and giggling, they announced, "No—NO RULES!!"

It wasn't hard to figure out what Rachel and Amanda meant. They had just started the first grade and it was like being in a straitjacket after the freedom of kindergarten. There were too many expectations, too many new rules: how to hold a pencil, where to put your hands, what you kept in your desk, what you brought home, how to write the alphabet and where and how to write your name and the date. School didn't feel like a place that they could just be themselves, according to their own timetable and own whims.

There are moments though when children need to tell us something that is not as direct or clear. We might hear about stomachaches or headaches, or become aware of a shift in usual demeanor from cheerful to prickly. I usually know something is up with my own daughters when I start feeling they are being too clingy, when I am being called an awful lot for what seem to me pretty minor things. I can remember a time when there seemed to be an unusual amount of fighting and bickering between the girls. They were more competitive with one another, vying to be the needier child. This was happening at a time that both my husband and I were absorbed in major work projects with deadlines that kept stretching out.

One afternoon I was slouched on the sofa, my head bent over the latest pile of papers. Out of the corner of my eye I saw Rachel approaching and as she did, one of those less than "perfectly motherly" reactions popped into my head. Irritated, I wondered, What is she going to ask for now? Sensing the potential for a cool reception, Rachel slowed her pace. To my astonishment, she reached in around my stack of work and with her little hand pressed my stomach firmly. Solemnly she asked, "You aren't having another baby are you?"

Hunched as I was over the sheaf of papers, scrutinizing them, laboring over them, I felt like a petty thief caught by bright flashlight, shocked and chastened. In my head I could hear the calm, moderated voice of the therapy teacher in me saying, "Sometimes a child acts up not for attention per se, not for a quantity of time that you can measure by the clock, but because she wants the parent to pay attention to something that the child cannot say herself, that sometimes the child does not know herself. It is a request for you to know that something needs to be listened to and understood, something that is too big or scary or amorphous for the child himself to put into words." This was one of those times. Something strange and nameless had entered our family life, something as demanding and as absorbing as a new baby, and neither Rachel nor Emily could figure out what made them feel as though the well of their mother's affection was mysteriously being dipped into. And so, they fought with each other instead. They picked the thief that was the closest at hand when they were really upset and angry with me, fearful that my work was taking their place in my heart.

———

Rachel and Emily weren't yet born when I met six-year-old Eleanor, who I remembered as one of my best and earliest teachers in how to listen for those things children say in actions and not words. Ellie was a sweet, compliant child who did well in school and was well liked by her teachers and the other students. She was four when her brothers Trevor and Charlie were born, and according to her parents, Paul and Maureen, she could not have been more delighted with their birth, acting very much the loving older sister toward them, solicitous and gentle. A bit suspicious of Ellie's easy acceptance of the twins, her parents made a point of dutifully asking how she was feeling. She always said, "good." This was a great relief to Paul and Maureen since six months after Charlie and Trevor were born, Maureen's dad, recently widowed, had come to live with them, a change that created even more stress and demands on them both.

Although Paul and Maureen had noted that Ellie was spending more time in front of the television and was invited less often by friends to play after school, they hadn't been concerned about her emotional adjustment until her annual pediatric visit. The pediatrician remarked that she had lost weight and seemed less lively than he remembered her, and suggested therapy. They weren't worried themselves about Ellie, but didn't object to her seeing me provided neither of them needed to be involved.

So it was, just Ellie and me. We met every Wednesday afternoon at four o'clock and sat face-to-face across a child-size table, usually drawing or molding tiny fruits and vegetables, animals and bugs from Play-Doh. We used these as props at the dinner party she staged every week where I was the guest and she was the hostess. Ellie would give me only the tiniest bit of food and drink and then I would have to watch her devour an enormous meal, course after hearty course. She would offer to share, but after I was glared at in the most intimidating way each time I accepted her offer, I finally learned it was necessary that I decline, insisting over the loud rumbling of my stomach (sound effects supplied by a ticking clock perched on my abdomen) that I was quite satisfied with my few morsels.

Eleanor's other favorite activity was to play birthday party. These were very fancy birthday parties she staged for herself with a construction paper birthday crown with stick-on gems and an imaginary four-layer birthday cake with fluffy pink frosting and purple and pink flowers. My part was to sing "Happy Birthday to You" very loudly and for as long as she waved her magic birthday spoon, smiling and nodding as regally as the Queen Mother herself.

Every few weeks, we had another party, which always began with a vigorous yank of the desk drawer containing her birthday finery and shouts of "Surprise!"

In all the weeks we spent together, Eleanor never said to me: "I feel rotten about having two new babies in my family," or "How come nobody is making a fuss about me?" Yet she could not have expressed these sentiments more clearly. They were all there: her sadness over losing her parents' active emotional involvement, her longing to rekindle their interest and excitement over her birth, and not just her brothers'. A sensitive and good-natured child, Ellie had intuitively understood her parents were overwhelmed first with the arrival of her brothers Charlie and Trevor, and then with her grieving grandfather. She had done her best not to give her parents any trouble. She was "fine." And for a time Paul and Maureen needed to believe that this was the whole story.

———

Contrary to the popular image of therapy, a therapist's objective is really not to achieve the brilliant insight, to pull back the curtain omnipotently on the patient's unconscious, but rather to offer a state of neutral attention and receptivity to the patient's emotions. Freud wrote, "The rule for the doctor may be expressed: He should simply listen, and not bother about whether he is keeping anything in mind. The therapist should suspend . . . judgment and give . . . impartial attention to everything there is to observe."

It had been important to Ellie that I just listen to the

feelings she worried about expressing to her parents. It helped that unlike Maureen and Paul I didn't have the responsibility of caring for a grief-stricken parent and two new babies, that it wasn't necessary to hide her true feelings from me. But it was equally important that Eleanor be encouraged to rediscover that her parents did not need to be protected from her feelings forever. She needed to be reassured that they would not love her less if they knew about them. After several months of therapy, I introduced the idea that Paul and Maureen would want to know about the things Ellie had been telling me during our therapy hours. I spoke about the therapy as being like a sleepover at a good friend's house, and like any sleepover, there comes a time to go home. In preparation for that change, I met with Ellie and her parents a few times and helped them talk over all the adjustments their family had been making. Without much prompting, Maureen and Paul told Ellie what a wonderful help she had been to them and how badly they had felt about always turning their attention last to her, always after her grandfather and after the babies. They promised her that it would be different, and for Ellie, that was everything that she needed to hear.

———

Often without even realizing it, parents expect their children, even young children, to tell them what they are thinking and feeling. I frequently encounter this expectation in parents who bring their children to therapy. They believe their failing as parents is their inability to get their child to tell them what is troubling him or her. They believe my special skill is getting children to talk, and feel sheepish and ashamed that a total stranger can be trusted by their child as an intimate and confidante. Parents ask me, "Did he tell you about . . . ? Or might remind their child to tell me about something or other that has taken place during the week, "Did you tell Dr. Ohye about . . . ?" Some bluntly ask their son or daughter, "What did you talk about in there?"

Many of the parents of the children I see in therapy have troubles of their own that get in the way of being sensitive to their child's nonspoken expressions; some have children who are temperamentally more difficult to read than others. But I have found that even your average parent with everyday children and everyday stresses also finds listening to a child who cannot be verbally expressive awkward, uncomfortable, confusing and tedious. They wish their child could or would just get to the point and say what is on his or her mind. And when he can't, even well-meaning parents can give up and tune out. Sometimes their attention drifts away from the child because they assume that a child talks about what's on his mind when he or she is ready. Sometimes parents worry that by waiting they are being manipulated for attention, and that too much attention is bad for children. Some have been taught that if it can't be spoken, it probably isn't all that important any way. The question, "Cat got your tongue?" even when asked with affection and mild joshing, captures as well as any this adult requirement that children present their wishes, thoughts and feelings in clear, forthright speech.

I should make clear that I do not think it wise for parents, even parents who happen to be therapists, to act like a therapist with their children. But I do think there is something of value to learn about how a therapist listens, nonreactively and nonjudgmentally. And I do think there is something instructive for all parents to consider in the therapist's willingness to listen for things children try to tell us that are not conveyed in speech.

To listen as therapists do is much more complicated if you are a parent listening to your own child. As my colleague Ellen points out, unlike parents, therapists do not have to decide when they can just listen, not instruct children about their behavior or impart important values. Extending this kind of quiet attentiveness is more difficult as parents because our relationships to our children are not formal or emotionally neutral. But it is also challenging because the value placed upon speech, words and talking is deeply embedded within Western culture. As Americans we prize free speech as a right of every citizen. In most middle-class American families, verbal self-assertion is viewed as a mark of healthy self-esteem and articulate speech as a reflection of intelligence. We teach our children the importance of "speaking one's mind" as a skill necessary for success, and believe that to speak with fluency and confidence is the mark of an individual of value and substance. We also tend to regard speech as a primary form of communication and of intimate connection between parent and child. At times these assumptions about talking can interfere with a parent's appreciation of things children express in ways other than by speaking.

We are gently encouraged to acquire this expectation about speech from the earliest age. In most communities, mothers are verbally interactive with their children even before they are born, believing educating children to be sensitive and responsive to speech is what good mothers are supposed to do. Expectant mothers are encouraged to talk to their babies in utero to familiarize them with our voices. After their birth, we talk more each day to our babies than do mothers in many non-Western cultures, and relate to them as though they are capable of talking with us, even though they are not. We create dialogues out of monologues by filling in what would be their part, for example, "How is my little guy? U-m-m, not so wonderful? You think I need to change your diaper? Ah, you're right. Let's go take care of that, shall we?" Here, it seems to me, are the roots of a relationship between mother and child in which talking to one another is a very important element in feeling closely connected.

Not only do we converse a good deal with our babies and toddlers, but our conversations have culturally distinctive characteristics. For example, our conversations are full of questions, three to four times as many questions as mothers in non-Western societies ask their children. We ask: How did you sleep? What would you like for breakfast? Does that feel too tight? We ask our children questions to which we already know the answer, such as, "What color is this? What letter is this? What's your name? What do we call (pointing to her nose, for example) this? We assume we must verbally direct their attention to interesting and stimulating events in the environment around us.

Psychologists who study the mother-child relationship cross-culturally suggest this pattern of dialogue between American mothers and their children prepares U.S. children for the interactions that take place between teachers and students in school. It promotes a child's "readiness" for the structure and expectations of the typical American classroom, and its reliance on verbal explanation ("Hold one shoelace in each hand, then . . ."), verbal testing ("How many days in the week?") and verbal reinforcement ("You did that beautifully)."

By responding to our infants' and young children's speech with speech of our own, we are facilitating their intellectual and social development, and preparing them for the kind of interaction that they will encounter in the environments outside the family, especially school and the workplace. Our pattern of interactions conveys to the infant a basic rule about social relationships, "You say something. Then I say something." Children inevitably learn that being spoken to is a very important way that mothers communicate their interest and attention, and it seems to me, their love.

Perhaps because of my native discomfort with talking, I find it very interesting that parents in other parts of the world place much less emphasis on speech as communication and an avenue of interpersonal connection and intimacy than we do. Gusii mothers of eastern Kenya, for example, think talking to babies a "waste of time." Gusii children learn to talk not by responding to their mother's verbally guided instruction or by conversing with her, but by watching and listening to others. Mothers in several African-American communities in Louisiana and working-class Carolina also do not emphasize verbal proficiency as a valuable developmental accomplishment in their children. Quite remarkably, and to the contrary, children in these communities are not encouraged either to initiate or take part in conversations with adults. They are instead encouraged to sit very quietly and listen to adults talk for up to three hours at a time. In fact, these children hold their parents' attention for longer periods when they do not speak at all.

Cross-cultural scientists suggest that speech as a form of interpersonal connection is more likely to develop in communities that separate children from the world of adult activity, and that also do not encourage a lengthy period of physical closeness between mothers and children. In some cultural communities mothers carry their children on their backs, in slings and other devices designed to keep them in physical contact, well into toddlerhood, and offer the breast freely to calm and comfort. In contrast, most middle-class American children are separated from parents for long periods of time each day—for sleep, for school and for activities arranged for the child's

enrichment and pleasure, activities that often do not involve parents, but parental surrogates. These are child-
rearing practices consonant with the developmental and
cultural goal of a child's early autonomy and self-reliance.
In the face of the culturally prescribed practice of repeated
physical separations of children from their parents, talking becomes a vital way to sustain a sense of the ongoing
connection between mothers and children.

However, in cultures where children are integrated
into the world of adult economic and social activity
more fully than in our own, and where babies and young
children are rarely physically apart from their primary
caregivers, there arises the possibility that other forms
of communication will assume greater prominence—
sounds, for example, as well as nonvocal forms of interaction such as touch, gestures, gaze and body position.
These nonlinguistic ways of communicating take the
place of words as the natural "vocabulary" in the emotional dialogue between children and their mothers, and
afford a sense of intimacy between mother and child that
is not as heavily dependent on speech as is the case in
our own.

———

Perhaps more than any other cross-cultural scholar, developmental psychologist Barbara Rogoff has elegantly and
persuasively documented how these structural differences
in childcare arrangements are associated with different
patterns of communication between children and their
parents. In a widely cited study of four communities (a

Mayan Indian town in Guatemala, a middle-class urban group of families in the United States, a tribal village in India, and a middle-class urban neighborhood in Turkey) she and her colleagues have captured and vividly described cultural variations in the role talking plays in the relationship between parents and their toddler children.

In studying these four communities, the researchers conducted and videotaped lengthy interviews in the homes of fourteen families in each of these four communities. They asked, among other things, about the family's caregiving and social network, the toddler's usual feeding and dressing routines, the kinds of games their child enjoyed, and how the caregiver taught the child what he or she was allowed to do and how to treat others. In addition to the parents' responses to the interview questions and the researchers observations of feeding and dressing routines, parents were presented eight objects that were unfamiliar to the child, and asked to teach the child how to operate them.

The use of videotape to record all observations in the study allowed the researchers to conduct very fine-grained analyses of the interactions between children and their mothers. The comparisons between the middle-class mothers in Salt Lake City and the mothers of San Pedro, Guatemala yielded the main findings of the research. The observations of the teaching interactions with the novel objects revealed quite dramatic differences. In general, mothers in Salt Lake City talked much more to their toddlers than did mothers in San Pedro. The pattern of interaction between the U.S. mothers and their children emphasized vocabulary lessons in the form of asking the child to label objects, providing a running commentary on events in the environment, expanding the children's speech and playing language games that often involved test questions. When teaching her child how to operate the wooden jumping jack toy, the American mother produced a steady stream of verbal prompts and comments in her demonstration ("Oh, look! What's this? Is that a little man? He's dancing!").

The San Pedro mother, on the other hand, instructed her child completely nonverbally. The jumping jack was operated by holding a string attached at the top and simultaneously pulling a string attached to the bottom. Pulling the bottom string made the legs of the jack move up and down. To instruct her child how to use this toy, the mother in San Pedro first physically and firmly placed the child's hand on the top string. She moved that hand into a position that indicated that the child should grasp the bottom string, and then lightly tapped the child's arm to communicate that the bottom string needed to be gently and not vigorously pulled.

The research detailed other communicative behaviors that develop in a cultural context that does not rely primarily on speech. For instance, if the child in San Pedro needed clarification and direction, he or she did not cry out or ask verbally for help as the Salt Lake City toddler would, but simply gazed at the mother. Their mothers were observed to be "poised in readiness to assist" their toddlers and were highly skilled in their ability to attend to multiple, and often competing activities in their physical and interpersonal surroundings.

This was unlike the American mothers who focused their attention on one event at a time, typically not being aware of other events that were occurring simultaneously. The toddlers in San Pedro were already quite skillful at this, attending to competing events in the environment. The researchers noted that they shared their attention among simultaneously occurring events more often than did the mothers in Salt Lake City, a community with lesser emphasis on quiet observation and greater emphasis on attention guided by verbal cues.

In communities that consider keen observation at the center of their conception of maturity and intelligence, this kind of active, although silent, study of one's surroundings is not limited to early childhood, but continues across the lifespan. Field studies of learning in other cultures illustrate that it is possible to acquire a complex skill and an understanding of complex social interaction through observation alone, without actually participating in, or carrying out, a given task. Adults in Guatemala, for instance, learn to use a foot loom in weaving factories simply by sitting next to a skilled weaver, asking no questions and receiving no explanations. In the United States, Navaho mothers do not pass on the art of weaving by telling their daughters what to do. Rather, after a long period of active observation of the mother, the daughter one day announces, "I am ready. Let me weave."

———

I am especially fascinated by cross-cultural reports such as these because they remind me of aspects of my childhood that I had not paid much attention to or considered out of the ordinary. As a very young child my family was an integral part of my paternal grandparents' household. I spent a great deal of time with my grandparents, especially with my grandmother, who frequently took me to work with her at the family grocery store, the Alameda Market. The store was neatly divided into two domains. My grandfather spent his time in "the front," where activities such as checking out groceries, arranging the produce and preparing the meat counter took place. But my grandmother and I spent our time in "the back." This was where I played in the stockroom, surrounded by shelves that reached from the floor to the ceiling. They were filled with canned goods of every sort: peas, corn, beets and cut green beans I thought all grown by the Jolly Green Giant. There were stacks of Betty Crocker cake mixes, her smiling face gracing each box; jewellike jars of jams, preserves and jellies; and detergent boxes that made you sneeze if you sniffed too hard. The back was also where I learned to trim radishes, celery and carrots and, when I was old enough, to wash rice for the sushi my grandmother made and sold in the store.

Some say it takes twenty years to acquire enough experience to cook perfect rice, rice that is plump and tender, shiny and moist. My grandmother bought her rice in one-hundred-pound sacks that she stored in a large aluminum garbage can. The cover fit very snugly and when I tried to remove it, it regularly resisted my most determined yanking and pulling. The commotion this made usually brought my grandmother to my rescue, clucking and shaking her head in amusement. Then, with a practiced motion, she rocked the lid off, inching it up, her fingertips curled under the rim, first one side and then the other. I could see the pearly surface of the rice, the plastic measuring cup nestled in it, usually half full. According to my grandmother, it was important to empty the cup out before measuring. So I'd give it a sharp shake to remove the few stubborn grains that clung to the sides.

We washed the rice in the same pot every morning. It was heavy, gray and cast iron with smooth, cool sides. I would hold it under the tap in the sink, my grandmother to my right, and fill it with a blast of cold water. When I was first learning, I scrubbed as though removing a stubborn stain, and loved to watch the water slosh up and over the sides of the pot, the rice rising on the swells and dropping into the sink.

My grandmother stopped me by putting her hand lightly on my wrist. She waited until the water was a calm, flat surface, then put her hand, slightly cupped, into the water and moved it slowly, unhurriedly, the grains following, as though subjects in a royal procession. As they moved, they floated out of the first powdery layer of rice bran, turning the water milky. My grandmother poured this dirty water out, opened the tap, and filled the pot with water again. I watched the water flow over her palm then along the interior wall and seep between the grains of rice until it rose an inch or so above them. She turned the rice once again and then drained the water, each repetition lifting off another white coat. She did this until the water was clear, unclouded; the rice, tiny moon white pillows. Then she covered the pot and let the rice rest.

Except for the running water and the rhythmic swish of the rice against the sides of the pot, my grandmother conducted this lesson silently. She gave no verbal directions, no words of praise, encouragement or correction. When I was young I accepted this as a condition of our relationship because she didn't speak English, and I didn't speak Japanese. In spite of the linguistic chasm between us, she would on occasion speak to me in Japanese even though I couldn't understand her. I knew she was disappointed about my not learning how to read, write and speak her native language as her own children had by attending Japanese language school. Perhaps she believed that by some magical combination of exposure, will and love, I would understand her anyway.

So when she talked to me, I listened to her murmur, her voice soft and low, and strained to make out the sounds that were just that, just a string of sounds, moving up and down, going slow, going more quickly, listening to the rise and fall and the few words that I did recognize, "Isn't that so?" "Good" "Just right." I listened for pleasure, approval, discomfort, excitement and apprehension in her voice. I heard clucks and clicks and the barely exhaled breath from her pursed lips. I studied her face and gestures and watched her body sway or tense or soften.

At the time I felt puzzled, and then as I got older, put upon, by my grandmother's determination to speak to me in a language I did not understand. It strikes me now that these were my first lessons in listening for things that are not in the words themselves. I learned that words are not the only medium of connection to someone that you love. Through the hours of companionable silence I shared with all four of my grandparents, planting flowers, picking cherries, in the car being driven to my music lessons, learning to cook and sew, I absorbed a different sense of how people who love one another communicate. I absorbed a sentiment and feeling about silence as more than its English dictionary meaning of "the absence of speech," as a state closer to its meanings in Japanese— serenity, pensiveness, vigilance and grace.

I don't consider this countercultural aspect of my growing up, or that of the Mayan community of San Pedro and the black American families in Louisiana, as representing a superior way of life or a superior way of conducting relationships. I am, after all, a middle-class American mother with children who will need to know how to speak up and tell others what exactly is on their minds. But I am grateful to have this knowledge about this other state of connection to another, a way to feel close to someone that is not so dependent on talking. It helps me remember that while we become who we are in part in response to the cultural models around us, we do not necessarily have to be limited or constrained by those patterns. It reminds me that how we think, act and feel as parents, and how we understand and act toward our children reflect a particular cultural context rather than some absolute and universal vision.

———

Even with all the self-doubt that my "little problem" with speaking caused me as a young therapist, all in all, I am glad I traveled a more circuitous route to get to where I am now. I'm glad because I think I learned a valuable lesson that I'm not sure I would have learned any other way. I learned that as much as my own native comfort in relationships is rooted in silence and not in speech, it is possible to extend oneself beyond the boundaries of personal comfort and learn to speak to someone in a language of relatedness that is not one's own. To listen and speak in another language of love.

LESSONS ON LOOKING

Land lies in water; it is shadowed green.
Shadows, or are they shallows, at its edges
showing the line of long sea-weeded ledges
where weeds hang to the simple blue from green.
Or does the land lean down to lift the sea from under,
drawing it unperturbed around itself?
Along the fine fan sandy shelf
is the land tugging at the sea from under?

Elizabeth Bishop, from "The Map"

GOODNESS AND SHAME

At a dinner meeting recently my friend David was show-ing us photographs of his newborn daughter, Lillian. It was so clear that he knew every line and indentation and curve on his daughter's tiny pink face. His own face was aglow, the circle of friends and colleagues gathered around him, admiring and congratulatory. All our oohing and aahing must have made David self-conscious because he suddenly and quite sheepishly exclaimed, "Gosh, I do sound like a new father don't I?" But none of us cared. We were overjoyed for him, remembering how we had been just as smitten with our new babies. Staring at Lillian brought back memories of the days when a creature ac-tually no more fascinating than, as my friend Cutler af-fectionately remarks, "a small meatloaf," was the most riveting sight in the entire universe. Every yawn, every stretch, every sweet exhalation was a fresh enchantment.

It was so different, looking at Emily and Rachel as newborns. Emily had a head of luxurious black hair and the delicate tracings of eyebrows and dark eyelashes. Rachel, born three weeks early, had none of these. Watching her features emerge was like watching a tree in springtime—the pale, barely visible green haze as it first begins to send out its leaf buds, gradually giving way to a glorious verdant crown. I have loved looking into those two faces ever since, watching them change, growing familiar with the expressions that are uniquely theirs, and realizing how often they have shown me feelings that they could not express verbally: the discomfort of hunger or fatigue, surprise and pain at those awful kindergarten immunizations, pride injured from a fall off the bicycle and hurt and anger at a friend who has broken a promise.

Social psychologists have studied the face as a mirror into human emotions for over thirty years. Certain emotions are universal—joy, fear, anger, sadness, shame, guilt, disgust—although the social cues that trigger them, and the ways people are taught to manage these emotions socially, can vary from culture to culture. Humans seem to be biologically inclined to look at other human faces. Human infants, for example, are from a very early age sensitive to facial expression. By the time babies are three months old, they can tell the difference between expressions of positive and negative emotion. By six or seven months, they are able to discriminate between different kinds of negative emotions such as anger and fear. Research has also shown that from as early as ten weeks babies begin to communicate some of the universal emotions, joy, sadness and anger, through changes in their facial expression.

Therapists also study faces, but in a different way. We observe faces in relationship to what patients say and do. We look at expressions, but also at discrepancies between what is said and what the facial expressions reveal about thoughts and feelings. Sometimes the look on a face, like a picture, *is* worth a thousand words. I was reminded a few years ago however that such attention for a therapist is not always automatic, that we aren't always tuned into the right channel. That reminder came when a young colleague Karen asked me to observe her therapy with a patient she felt increasingly baffled and frustrated by. Her patient, a five-year-old girl named Heather, had been removed from her parents' custody because of their heavy drug involvement. Karen felt Heather liked her and enjoyed coming to therapy, but was resisting Karen's every effort to explore meaningful and relevant material. Karen thought Heather needed to talk abut the abuse that she probably suffered at the hands of her father, the neglect she experienced with both parents and the continuing ambiguity about whether she would ever live with them again.

Sitting in the darkened observation room, I waited for Karen and Heather to begin their session. Heather was wearing jeans, sneakers and a T-shirt with rainbow-colored hearts printed across the front. Short and plump, she looked around the room before settling into the chair by the desk. Karen took her seat in the large, padded swivel chair and asked how Heather's week had gone. Heather answered "good," and although Karen didn't say anything, I could see her lips retreat into a thin line, and the muscles in her neck were suddenly more visible. Karen asked what Heather wanted to do and when Heather said, "I don't know," Karen sighed and said, "You like to draw. Why don't we do that."

Reaching for the paper and box of markers, Karen began to ask more about Heather's week. Had she seen her mother? Her father? What had they done during their visit together? How did Heather feel about seeing them? Heather's black marker was moving randomly across the paper, and I could see that she was biting her lip from the inside. Soon she was shifting her weight from side to side in her chair, and it became clear that the conversation was beginning to overwhelm her.

Children in therapy are very good at distracting themselves from uncomfortable thoughts and feelings. They twirl in the desk chair, demand to go to the bathroom, insist they must be on their hands and knees to find a missing game piece, take a stapler and punch staple after staple, like an automaton, into pieces of paper. Heather didn't do any of these, but after scribbling and wiggling for a while she told Karen she hadn't had anything to eat since lunch at school, and wanted to go to the vending machine to buy some candy. Karen hesitated and then countered with, "Okay, but then let's try and talk some more about your week."

Karen was right about Heather, she did enjoy coming to see her, but at the same time she seemed tense. I thought Karen was struggling to allow herself simply to be with her patient, looking at what she was doing, listening to what she was saying and, then the hardest thing of all, trusting that it would make sense in its own good time. She was trying too hard to make her idea of "good therapy" happen, and that idealized goal was getting in the way of Heather's becoming comfortable enough to communicate what she needed Karen to understand about her.

This observation was not particularly brilliant. Every therapist makes this mistake and makes it more than once. Like any other skill, therapy requires practice; with enough practice a therapist learns to figure out when she's making this error and how to get back on track. I still remember making the same mistake with a little girl named Ronnie. She was seven at the time. Ronnie's father had died the year before after a long illness, and her mother thought that even though Ronnie wasn't having any problems, talking to a therapist would be a good idea.

Almost as soon as we were in my office for our first session, Ronnie picked up the doctor's kit and the large rag doll. I couldn't believe my luck. I was sure we would immediately get to the feelings I presumed were the most important to this child: loss, sadness, anger. I can remember excitedly rummaging around in the doctor's kit for the stethoscope, putting the plastic ear pieces in my own ears and gingerly laying the bell-shaped piece onto the doll's chest. "I wonder what her heart is telling us?" I asked. To my disappointment, Ronnie didn't answer my question. I must have expected she would say without hesitation, without any reluctance, "She misses her father." So I tried again. And again she didn't say anything. This, I realize now, was her answer. But because I believed I knew exactly what needed to be done to restore this child's emotional well-being, I wouldn't accept that answer. Instead, thinking for a bit, then feeling pretty pleased with myself, I tried a different tack. Holding the stethoscope out to her I asked, "Maybe you can hear something that I can't?"

Ronnie's answer was quite empathic then. I guess it had to be since I was being so unbelievably dense. She scrambled up from the spot on the floor where we were sitting, quickly surveyed the contents of the office, and pulled Candy Land off the bookcase, announcing that she wanted to "play with Princess Lolly." Being a considerate child, she didn't add, "INSTEAD OF YOU," although she probably felt it. It wasn't until I reviewed the videotape of my session with my supervisor that I registered Ronnie's reaction. I had scared her. Her face, sad and frozen in a polite little smile would have told the most casual observer that she couldn't handle the frontal assault I was making on her most tender feelings. But I missed it because I was so thoroughly convinced I knew what was best for her. My conviction was so compelling that it was impossible for me to see that it was pushing Ronnie away from me, and making it harder for her to trust me with her feelings.

———

Parents, like therapists, also have visions of what is good and helpful for children. We want to help them become individuals we take pride in, admire and enjoy. For most of us we hope they will be happy, self-sufficient, economically comfortable and successful, have opportunities to develop their talents and gifts, and perhaps be involved with a spiritual community. In other words, we want them to adopt and live by the values that we hold dear. While we can love and accept their foibles and eccentricities within the family, we feel a responsibility to prepare them for the challenges and judgment of the outside world. But there are times when a parent's need for affirmation of a much cherished vision of the moral and upright life interferes with his or her clear-sighted appreciation of a child. Parents must temper this need for self-affirmation with an appreciation and acceptance of the differences children inevitably have with them, and as they mature into adulthood, to develop an attitude that encourages children to define their own sense of the upright life. It has seemed to me that the more insistently parents cling to a fixed vision of the admirable, principled life and turn a blind eye to what Sara Ruddick has called, "alternative excellences," the more they close off the self-reflection essential to a trusting and honest relationship with children.

I don't make this assertion lightly. To open oneself to

self-scrutiny can feel wrenching and deeply emotionally challenging. It can mean questioning something that feels fundamental to one's identity, questioning the actions of those who were so instrumental in forging that identity and the values that anchor it to family, town, social strata, and identify one as a member of a particular time, place and historical epoch.

Early in my training I worked with a young anorexic girl whose parents grappled with this challenge. They were a couple who seemed unable to imagine an alternative conception of the admirable life even though their child's health was at stake, and even though were good, well-intentioned parents who loved their child very, very much. My patient's name was Alicia, and she was fifteen years old. Two years before our therapy began she had noticed her tummy spilling softly over the top of her pants. She stood herself in front of her parents' bedroom mirror, turning slowly, examining herself from all angles. She was not slender and lithe. Her friends had begun to boast of wearing size zero; she wore size four. Not fat, but not thin. Innocently, she eliminated sugar from her diet. Then fat. She had managed to get her diet down to water, skim milk, an occasional piece of fruit, a salad now and then if one of her parents insisted. Her best days were the ones she didn't have to eat anything at all. The days when she could ignore the hunger, rise above it, and feel ethereal, ascetic, clean. It made her feel giddy to think that air was all she really needed. Her grandfather used to tell her stories about Marie Curie. He would describe how she could study for hours on end in a cramped heatless room ignoring her hunger and the cold. By will alone Marie Curie transcended the demands of her body. She had become Alicia's inspiration.

Alicia would not say so, but it was obvious she did not want to talk with me. The therapy was her parents' idea, not hers. Each week she would sit in her usual chair, by the desk, the right side of her body pressed flat against its side, to make herself smaller, to merge into something else, to give herself support. My sense of that changed from week to week. Her face was pale, and dark circles pooled beneath her large brown eyes. Her dark hair tumbled around her face and down to her shoulders, hair she had hated ever since she could remember because it set her apart from the others in the family. She was the youngest and the only girl. Her older brothers were away at school, one at Brown, one at Stanford. She adored them, but hated that they were so brilliant, so accomplished and confident. She emphasized that everyone in her family was perfect, except for her. She felt very fortunate to have such a wonderful family. They loved her and she loved them. But she wasn't perfect like they were. She had to work at everything.

Alicia's sense of insufficiency pervaded our relationship, too. She was sure she was not talking right, that I was judging her inferior somehow. In the beginning, she had no idea how she might be failing in her role as the patient, but she was certain she was anyway. She berated herself for not being insightful enough, not reflective enough, not able to feel what I thought she should be feeling. She watched me closely for clues. She would say, "I'm numb. What should I be feeling?" Yet her anger filled the silent room most afternoons. It was so intense it was even hard for me to talk at times. I would have to tell myself to take a deep breath. It happened when I seemed to be listening with less than my full attention, halfheartedly. In those moments, she would stiffen and retreat even as she sat stone still, unmoving. Her eyes would crinkle slightly at the corners, and her tone became icy. She was furious when my frailties took me away from her. I would tell her I felt sad to think only the impossible, only perfection, brought her peace and happiness, and contentment. Only then would her expression soften.

————

Although Alicia's parents were in treatment with another therapist, they would meet with me periodically, but separately because they were in the process of being divorced. Like most parents who enlist the aid of a therapist, they believed Alicia shared all her secrets with me and confided to me all her disappointments in them. They were not accustomed to being seen in a bad light, and so they wanted me to know that they had always loved Alicia. They were warm, concerned, generous, kind parents, and had always been.

Alicia lived with her mother Janna, and visited with her father Stephen every Saturday and alternating Sundays. Since moving out of the house, Stephen liked to take Alicia to his favorite restaurants, refusing to adhere to the diet the doctor had prescribed for his heart. When they ate together she would refuse the morsels he offered from his plate. This was another rejection, but he firmly believed Alicia was unaware of his hurt feelings. He was absolutely certain he had very skillfully kept Alicia from knowing his true feelings about Alicia's illness and about Alicia's mother. He and his ex-wife made a point never to argue in front of the children, or to show anger toward one another. He took pride in the fact that theirs was always a very civilized home.

Alicia's mother Janna was a tall, slender blonde, just as Alicia had described her. She adored her children and was thrilled to have a girl after the two boys. For many years they were a very happy family. Stephen devoted himself to his work and Janna was devoted to the children. She baked the cookies for the PTA, sat on committees, attended parent-teacher conferences, carpooled, planned birthday parties, scheduled doctors' appointments, knew the names of friends and teachers and when, where and what time the next soccer or swim or tennis practice was. She always made sure everything was organized and smooth running. She had done everything she had believed good mothers must do for their children.

She had read somewhere that children can be derailed from their natural developmental course, from their destiny as strong, talented, healthy individuals by subtle assaults to the brain. Did I think something like that had happened to her beautiful little girl? She proposed to me, as a friend had to her, that a virus had "brushed" Alicia's nervous system and caused this terrible thing to happen. She wanted very much to believe this might be true. She found it "inconceivable" that someone could not explain to her what went wrong with her child. She subscribed to the view that everything in life had an explanation, that the correct explanation could be found with the right effort, and if one was smart enough.

Going back and forth between my work with Alicia and the periodic meetings with her parents, I slowly and tentatively pieced together a portrait of this family. Alicia had been the effervescent, rambunctious, expressive child. She hugged everyone and asked (shamelessly) to be hugged. She told her parents she loved them one hundred times for every time either of them said the same to her. When compared to her brothers and her parents, everything about her seemed excessive, immoderate, wild. That was okay. She was fine with it, really. She knew they loved her. That was all that should matter.

Then about the time she turned eleven, she felt something change. Or maybe it was no different; she was just old enough to begin to notice. Her mother's usual reminder to her father about taking rotaries more cautiously became more insistent, strident. Her father's infrequent and awkward expressions of affection toward her mother were quietly rebuffed, an averted face, a cringing withdrawal from his embrace. Mother seemed more concerned about her appearance, then lost some weight precipitously after a bout with the flu. She denied it, but Alicia could see she was elated. New clothes, a new look, a spring to her step. Invigorated by her latest professional project, she was suddenly away a lot for evening meetings.

Her father spent the time with Alicia, making a point of being home to help with her homework even though she did not need it, and was not accustomed to it. He seemed out of place at the kitchen table in the middle of the day. It was all too confusing and weird. Of course, her mother made sure everything was in order before she left the house. A note for Alicia, a reminder to her father about how to warm the dinner she had prepared, where to find the croutons for the salad and that there were minia-ture marshmallows if Alicia wanted hot chocolate after school. She never forgot a thing. Alicia told herself not to worry. She had wonderful parents. She read in some mag-azine that all parents begin to act differently when their children go off to college. Something called empty nest syndrome. But the nest wasn't empty. She was still around. Why did it feel like she wasn't supposed to be?

As soon as she had such thoughts, she reprimanded herself for imagining things, for being foolish and self-centered. She shouldn't expect things to revolve around her. Nothing had changed, really, she guessed. So what if her dad was around the house more, trying to teach her a "better way" to solve that last math problem or the "more precise" explanation for the results of her physics lab ex-periment. She complained once to her oldest brother, Ben, but he told her she was "too sensitive" and to humor "the old guy." For a while she followed his advice and was mostly okay during the day. But at night her dreams were full of fury. Her brothers screaming they wished she would disappear from the face of the earth. In these dreams, they leaned in very close making sure she could hear them, so close she felt every "p" and every "t" they spoke, tiny blows raining on her head. She woke up, feeling reamed out, limp. She added two miles to her usual five mile run and vowed to eat nothing that day.

Inside Alicia's world, there was no such thing as a harmless mistake, a simple oversight or omission. There was either perfection or chaos. She had to control everything: her needs, her emotions, her mind. She had always felt she was a flawed object requiring additional attention, not attention that was joyful and abundant, but attention that was full of private irritation that she was too much for them. She had to push away these feelings because they couldn't possibly be true. Her parents were never petty, cruel, angry, unkind, selfish; they were always perfect. She needed to show them she could be too, even if it killed her.

Bright and accomplished, Stephen and Janna spoke freely and with great concern about their children. It was clear that they loved Alicia very much. As a couple, they shared a vision of the proper, respectable life for children. They worked in perfect partnership to create a family that would not be judged as a family that was lacking in any way. The right community, the right friends, the right schools, the right upbringing. Orderly, predictable, safe, enriched, controlled. They believed this is what children need. But in this endeavor to prepare Alicia for the scrutiny of the world outside their family, they "never thought to reach out to her inner world." And when they tried, they could not do it without subtly imposing a sense of what the proper, expected and appropriate thoughts and feelings should be. "I know you are just so excited . . . I know you won't make a fuss . . . This is just perfect! You think so too, don't you?" As I got to know these parents it was clear that their own families had not prepared them to do otherwise. They were joined not merely by the vows of marriage, but by the convergence of their family histories.

———

As a girl, Janna watched her own mother scurry around an explosive, domineering husband, quieting their four children so as not to disturb him, "set him off" was the expression they used, when in fact her efforts were futile and unconnected to her husband's outbursts. She believed, as women had since the late nineteenth century, that her wifely duty was to create a perfect domestic sphere, a haven against the aggressive, competitive world of men. She cooked, she cleaned, she scrubbed, she met every need, she was "a saint," but still the tirades came, ruthless and unpredictable. They began with a reminder that he was a good provider; his father had not been; his mother suffered the humiliation of being the object of neighborhood gossip and rumor. She, on the other hand, had every comfort, every labor-saving device money could buy. He was fulfilling his responsibilities. If she could not, there must be something wrong with her. He left the room, the air quivering in the wake of the door's closing.

When Janna's mother emerged from the room, Janna was in hers, frightened and alone. She waited for the sound of her mother's light, even footsteps descending the carpeted stairs, and counted slowly to three—the time it took to walk through the dining room and into the kitchen. She listened intently for running water. And then it came, the slap, slap, slap of the mop on the immaculate linoleum floor.

Janna grew up fearful of the feelings her mother never expressed, and uncertain about how to express her own. She absorbed, as well, her father's terror of being mocked and ridiculed, of being looked upon by others as their social inferior. She was schooled to put her best face forward no matter what. This required her to be controlled, always composed, always better, because this was the only way to triumph over those wagging tongues, the only way to avoid being shamed and humiliated.

———

Stephen's father was a man of limited education. He owned a local tavern, and the family lived above it. His mother endeavored ceaselessly to make it a clean and respectable home for the three of them. Being an only child, he spent a good deal of time with her, and inherited his love of books and good music from her. She loved classical music and played her favorite operas every evening while his father was at work. He thought in retrospect to distract herself from the carryings on downstairs. She enveloped herself in the languages of high culture: Italian, German, French. Sometimes however the sound of brawling men, raucous laughter, cat calls and whistles escaped from below, through the floorboards, the radiators, up the back stairs, disturbing the fantasy of other circumstances, other associations, the fantasy of another self. "Degenerates," she would hiss. Her pride in him was Stephen's constant companion: pride in his intelligence, his abstinence, his gentility and eventually in his cultured friends. Her need that he be noble, gallant, flawless, elevated over the primitive world of his father was insatiable.

———

Like many young girls who develop anorexic symptoms, it was many months before Alicia began to get better. She faded in and out of phases of worrisome eating, a bad patch usually coinciding with a new development in the process of her parents' divorce. The turning point came, as often happens, in the form of a crisis. Janna and Stephen had grown impatient with Alicia's slow progress and requested a second opinion. The consultant recommended Alicia live apart from both of them. In his estimation, she needed to be in a more emotionally neutral place, some place, other than home. Stephen agreed with the recommendation, while Janna did not.

On the afternoon following the consultation, Stephen and Janna met with me. They looked grim and exhausted, their conflicts heightened by their differing responses to the consultant's assessment. Alicia joined her parents halfway through this meeting, the impasse between them hanging in the air. With a composure and directness I had not seen before she said, "Mommy, please don't let them send me away. I promise to be good. I promise to try harder" and began to cry. Neither parent moved. I started to say something, but before I could begin, Alicia repeated, "Please give me another chance. I know I can be a better person." Like winter breakup on a frozen pond, horror crept across Janna's face. At last she said in a choked whisper, "Oh, my god, what have we done?" her face no longer composed, mourning the losses that are the consequence of an unexamined vision of the admirable life.

————

One could say this is a cautionary tale about the pursuit of perfection, about mothers and fathers seeking the affirmation they need as good parents and admirable individuals, or about the havoc wreaked when the parental wish for a perfect child goes unchecked. Each version in its own way is true. But this is also a tale about shame and how even from the recesses in which it dwells it can animate our actions toward our children. We tend not to speak about such matters: shame, humiliation, degradation of the human spirit or the psychological toll they extract. We talk about being embarrassed or ashamed maybe, but rarely about being so reduced by another's pointed and unrestrained hatred or disdain that it erodes one's sense of worth as a member of the human race.

Psychologists have only recently begun to conduct empirical investigations on what are known as the "self-conscious" emotions: guilt and shame. Current psychological theory describes shame as an emotion caused by a person's negative self-evaluation. Although the terms "shame" and "guilt" are often used interchangeably, psychological studies demonstrate that they are quite different from one another. Guilt arises from negative evaluation of specific behaviors or transgressions, whereas with shame, no part of one's selfhood is spared negative judgment. Subjectively, guilt is uncomfortable; shame is acutely painful and overwhelming, an emotion accompanied by a sense of worthlessness, powerlessness and exposure.

The relative absence of scientific interest in shame as a psychological experience is striking. It is particularly interesting since Freud's earliest psychoanalytic explorations began with observations of his patients' memories of shameful experiences. His initial studies of hysteria were remarkable illustrations of the psychologically devastating effect of feelings of inferiority or rejection.

Once I began to give shame and what it does to people more serious consideration, I found myself moving out of the purely intrapsychic models of my training into ones that take geography, class, race and a nation's culture and history into account. I remembered mothers who had seemed controlling, nagging, overly involved, perfectionistic, and might even talk about themselves using these terms. I wondered how often in a day in their lives as mothers they were inexplicably enveloped by a memory of being shamed or of being hated, and, in that state, lost their sense of goodness. Allowing such thoughts into my understanding of myself as a mother, and of other mothers, I found other stories I had heard beginning to take on a new clarity. Some of them are just fragments, stories that you could hold in the palm of your hand.

———

One year, the week before Thanksgiving, I heard by e-mail from an old friend whose mother was as volatile as mine was serene: "I finally see that my mother rails and rails at her children until we can stand it no longer and we are forced to abandon her as she was abandoned in the war. This is something she has never been able to speak about. So my sisters and brothers and I can only guess at the horrors that revisit her. When we were children, her head would fill with thoughts of our unworthiness and our insufficiencies, and thus preoccupied, she was released, if just for a little while, from a lifetime of fearing her own."

———

Over lunch, a high-powered attorney in a prestigious Boston law firm confided to me that she found herself tugging at the hems of her teenage daughter's dresses and skirts. She didn't do this because she feared, as I first thought to myself, the predatory glances of men and boys, but because to her way of thinking it was not necessary to dress fashionably. Why not? I asked. Is it because you don't like to see her buckling under to peer pressure? No, she said, I just want her to learn it isn't necessary to be happy. She laughed, her eyes darting away from mine. It seems her mother survived the Holocaust by convincing herself that happiness was irrelevant to life, that it was completely frivolous. And now she was herself a mother, afraid her only child would grow dependent on happiness. When she had this thought, she felt faint and tugged harder.

———

Mary was a recently divorced woman in her mid-twenties with two children. She came to therapy to talk about the unforeseen incompatibilities of her interracial marriage. Her family, church and friends had gotten her through the separation and divorce, but she felt certain they could not help her with what was left. What was left, she told me, was, "all this stuff, private stuff I never knew I felt about being black and about his being white." Mary hadn't given much thought to what it would be like to be married to Karl. She got pregnant on the eve of their college graduation, and when she told Karl, he was overjoyed. They were in love and looked at this turn of events as a sign that they were meant to be together forever.

Mary told me about their first major argument, "the beginning of the end," she said. It happened on an outing with their newborn son. Karl had planned a hang-loose, make-it-up-as-we-go excursion into the country. They would just jump into the car with plenty of diapers and head for the nearest highway. As the miles mounted and their location became more and more unfamiliar, she kept pestering him with the same question, "Do you know where we are?" She did not know why, but she felt her panic rising until, confused and shaking, she was screaming, "Do you want to kill us?!" Stunned, they eventually made up and chalked it up to postpartum depression. But after Karl and the baby were asleep, Mary revisited her fear and found it had revised itself in the hours that had passed since her outburst. She did not fear for her husband's life; he was white. He would be protected; he would be safe out there where she knew no one and no one knew her. No, she feared for her life and that of her beautiful baby boy with the silky mahogany skin. She had married believing in a color-blind relationship. Everyone was alike underneath. That's what they had both been taught. "Well," she told me, "I discovered it wasn't true."

———

My own encounter with shame like this happened one morning the year Emily began middle school. Just as she was leaving the car I managed to tap her fingernails lightly. They were too long. I knew right away I had made a mistake. The happy, eager expression had vanished from her face. Before I could say anything, she slipped out of the car and into the throng of children milling around the nondescript building that is her school, and I was left with that lingering image of her face, crestfallen, hurt, perplexed. Inching along in the stream of cars, past the cafeteria, the gym, the row of empty bike racks, I kept seeing her face.

I don't have much trouble voicing my outrage when I think Emily has been unfairly hurt by someone. But it is harder to keep from turning away from that face of anger or sorrow or hurt when I know that I am responsible for those feelings. I'm sure some would think I made a mountain out of a molehill. And were it not for Emily's natural sweetness I might not have given it another thought. But I've noticed that quiet children can lose out on their fair share of attention and justice in families. You know, those children who by their nature are accepting and tolerant, the ones who absorb the slights and injustices and give others the benefit of the doubt. That's the kind of person Emily is.

So out of respect for her kindheartedness, I asked myself why I had needed to reach out and adjust just this one little thing about her. It was one of those small interactions that on the outside are "nothing," but on the inside, feel like a thunderclap. What was that tap about? I am too critical . . . I place too much emphasis on appearance . . . I have difficulty separating from my child and must introduce conflict to cover up the pain of being apart . . . Her budding womanliness frightens me. None of them captured the intensity of my reaction, though. It felt as if some unseen demon had plopped itself between us, grabbed my hand and made me tap that slender finger. It felt irresistible, and it asserted itself as more important than my child's feelings and spirit as she made her way into another day of her life.

I cannot tell you when the thought first formed that my action might be a tendril reaching from the past into my present, a tendril about shame and humiliation. The mind truly is a peculiar beast, taking in and letting go fragments of a life's puzzle enigmatically and unexpectedly. Some things are not released until our children move along and require new things of us, and as we respond to their maturing, we discover new aspects of ourselves, aspects connected to memories we would rather not encounter. Memories, bone memories, dream memories, memories that inhabit us without our knowing it, rearing up and obscuring what is on a child's face.

What I had to let myself imagine was not just a crisp winter day, but the precise moment on that day when my grandmother, an unassuming forty-two-year-old woman raising seven children in her abiding Christian faith, learned that unseen, important others hated her, thought she was dangerous and bad, and would soon be sending her away, a postal tag with the family number, #xxxxx, secured to a buttonhole in her winter coat, fluttering in the wind. And then I thought again about that tap to my oldest daughter's fingernails, of the three generations of her mother's Japanese history converging in that single, acute moment of our relationship. It contained an exhortation, the outlines of a fragile ploy against the other's shaming, hate-filled glance: Do not give them anything to ridicule, mock or detect as a failing. Be above reproach. Be good.

––––

On the shelves of the bookcase in our living room I keep small treasures friends and students have given me over the years. Behind the glass-front doors you can see a pair of tiny hand-carved turtles from Southeast Asia, symbols of longevity; a slender statue of a human figure from Greece; and a graceful wing-shaped letter opener made in Haiti by an artist I have never met named Marie Celestin. Among them on the top shelf to the left is a small square ceramic box sent to me by my e-mail friend. It is pale blue and cool to the touch. Although I have spent a good deal of time looking at the dark blue brushstrokes on its cover, it is hard to make out what they are supposed to be. This is because what I see is just a small piece of a larger image.

The cover is from a piece of pottery destroyed during Mao Tse-tung's Cultural Revolution. Once a bit of debris, a modern Chinese craftsman has reclaimed it as a thing of beauty and of contemplation. If you close your eyes and pass your hand lightly over its surface you can feel a hint of the pot's curve. The edges, which must have been sharp at one time, are framed in silver filigree now, row upon row of delicate silver dots, slanting like a warm rain.

It struck me recently that my friend has fashioned the same kind of beauty and purpose in her relationship with her sons that this gift reflects. She has found her way to soften her own sharpness, the harshness she can slip into from time to time. At one time it seemed an understandable emotional inheritance from her mother, but I don't see it that way now. These days it seems more the emotional legacy of a war to suppress all but a single ideal. I admire her way of being a mother. She makes a point to say to her sons, "Yes, you are right," when they are, and she is not. She thanks them for reminding her when she needs to "give it a rest." Her younger son, always skilled at imitating those sounds that make trains and planes and battles come alive, softly creates a whip flicking the air, and she laughs and sighs and starts all over again. They are the sort of sons who take their mother shopping for a new coat and don't mind if she takes a long time to find the right one.

———

All through high school my friend kept at me to stand up and make myself known. She'd say, "You have got to stick your hand up there and start waving it!" So while it was not the most incisive translation of her advice, I thought she'd probably be pleased to hear that when Emily asked to read part of this chapter as I was working on it one afternoon, I let her.

I didn't know if she would remember that morning and that tap to her finger. Wondering and waiting, I watched her eyes move across the page. It could not have been more than a few minutes, but it felt like an eternity. She put the last page down and as she did said, "I remember that time. I thought you were teasing me, making fun of me, but I didn't know why." She hugged me reassuringly, the kind of hug I once believed only children, not mothers, needed. It told me she understood and forgave me. I was glad to have been able to remember, however imperfectly and belatedly, glad I could show her that I had been looking at her after all.

NATURE AND NURTURE

I've been thinking a lot lately about the father of a patient I know. The patient, a little boy named Tyler, sees a young therapist I consult to. Tyler's father is a tall, trim, black man who was born and raised in Barbados. His father was a native of Barbados, his mother from the Punjab region of India. How Tyler's dad came to live in the United States I don't know. He wasn't much interested in talking about himself the one time he agreed to meet with Tyler's therapist. He arrived for that meeting wearing black boots and jacket, gun and holster; he was on his way to work and did not plan to stay long. He came to let the therapist know that contrary to what the doctors, the school and his child's mother think, his son did not have an attention deficit disorder. "In my country, there is no such thing as ADD; no such thing as hyperactivity. Children do not need to take drugs to pay attention or to control themselves."

Tyler's father went on to say he does not believe there is anything wrong with his son that a little discipline and structure in the household would not immediately improve. When his son is with him, his behavior is perfectly controlled, not "hyper" or inattentive or unresponsive, ever. He believes American doctors invented "attention deficit disorder" as an excuse for lazy parents, and as an excuse to give drugs. In his opinion, Tyler's mother is at fault. She is lax, undisciplined and cannot run a home with sufficient clarity and consistency of routine to teach this child self-control. Under his watch, his son is fine, polite and obedient. To his way of thinking, this disproved the diagnosis. Then rising from his seat, he gave a curt nod of his head, thanked the therapist for his time, and announced he saw no need to speak with him again.

I do not know the history and culture of Barbados well enough to say whether Tyler's father's viewpoint is representative of the expectations parents in Barbados have for their children. The few studies that address Caribbean parental values and child-rearing practices are limited to families living in poverty. These studies suggest that in these families parents emphasize obedience as a characteristic closely linked to economic survival, and as a result they are more likely to use physical punishment to discipline their children. According to cross-cultural psychologists, children born into poverty or politically oppressed groups must learn not to resist authority as a matter of survival. The jobs available to them, for example, are likely to be ones where workers are subject to strict control and supervision. Under such circumstances, obedience becomes a personal skill that can determine whether one keeps a job and supports a family. In more extreme political situations, obedience can become an adaptation necessary to avoid being imprisoned or killed. Perhaps when Tyler's father was a boy, this kind of disciplined compliance and self-control were required of him. He now insists his son learn the same kind of self-control because it is what was expected of him as a child. For him, it is what feels right and proper.

These days the front page of the *New York Times* and the cover of *Time* magazine declare that genes account for more than the color of our children's eyes and how tall they will grow to be. Shyness, pessimism, risk-taking, aggression, aspects of personality we usually believe result from a child's interaction with parents, are regarded instead as behavioral expressions of their genetic inheritance. The six o'clock evening news recently concluded with a human interest story of identical twins separated at birth, reared apart in very different family environments, reunited as adults who have each married a woman named Mary, fathered two boys and a girl, labored at the same job, wear khaki pants and button-down white shirts on the weekends and sing bass in the church choir. It was another proclamation of nature's triumph over nurture. More and more it seems the message is that children are, and then become, who they are, not because of parents' effort to direct, guide and shape their children's behavior, but because of the genes their children inherit from them.

In such an intellectual climate, it doesn't seem possible that any reasonable man or woman would refuse to admit that a child's development is shaped and therefore is sometimes compromised by his or her biological endowment. Most parents I work with are greatly relieved to learn that an aberrant neurological process is responsible for their child's problem behavior, and not their parenting. Grateful for this information, they are able to stop berating themselves as ineffectual mothers and fathers and, with enough time, release themselves from the dispirited conclusion that their child is incorrigible, impossible, or just a bad seed. Tyler's father's opinion seems outdated and uninformed, his faith in the overriding power of a parent to influence a child's character, backward and unsophisticated.

For these reasons, I think the therapist consulting me assumed I would roll my eyes at Tyler's father's opinion and align myself unambiguously with those who give greatest weight to nature rather than nurture in a child's development. The truth is I couldn't. Not because the diagnosis didn't seem clear, but because I have felt this same theme, nature versus nurture, weave in and out of my dealings with my daughters, and watched it exert its influence in the families of friends just as forcefully as in those of the patients I have worked with. I have watched its expression, not in large, dramatic showdowns like the one created by this father, but in small, fleeting moments between mothers and their children.

I remember standing in the kitchen of a close friend with her school-age daughter whom I had known since the time she was only a few months old. The kitchen was warm and fragrant with the aroma of the soup we were making. My friend M.E., short for Mary Ellen, had given eight-year-old Laura the job of slicing the bread, a thick, crusty peasant loaf that she always served when I came over for a meal. Usually I cut the bread, but that night M.E. was eager that Laura take part in the dinner preparations. Laura was obviously thrilled to have achieved this new maturity in her mother's eyes, and she raced over to the breadboard. Raising herself on tiptoe she grasped the loaf firmly and with the knife poised just right, began to saw back and forth. After a minute or so, her smile disappeared and her face clouded over with frustration. The knife blade was much too dull, and she was much too short. Distressed, Laura called to her mother, "It's too hard, Mommy." Her mother replied sharply, "It's nothing that a little effort won't overcome! Persevere, Laura, persevere!"

Perhaps I note moments that reveal a parent's effort to mold a child's character more than most because I live in a place where this imperative is deeply embedded in its history. It is a history powerfully reshaped by seventeenth-century English Protestants and their geographic search for a home in which they could worship "purely and unceasingly." The town I live in is connected by a simple two-lane rise curving gently over a narrow inlet of the Atlantic Ocean to the town where the Salem witch trials took place. My children have taken regular field trips with their schools to locations significant in the Puritan settlement of New England. Each time, we crowd together on a bare dirt floor, teachers, parents and twenty lively, chattering children, under a thatched roof that was once a place of worship. The guide, accustomed to the ways of first graders, waits until the last shuffling feet settle and then tells us that we are standing where five- and six-year-old Puritan children stood long hours on the Sabbath. Their clothes were hot and scratchy and cumbersome. Yet they stood through the service without moving and without uttering a single sound. They did not even yawn. We are, grown-ups and children alike, awestruck as we contemplate this gulf between then and now. The freedom of movement, thought, speech and impulse of our children is suddenly no longer an immutable given about the nature of a child, but a convention of the time and place in which we live. We must think about a time right here in America, not on the other side of the globe, when the standard of behavior Tyler's father spoke about was the rule, not the exception. And the parent who required it was viewed not as despotic, but as responsible, loving and pious.

Every conscientious Puritan parent lived in fear of failing in his duty to educate his children for "right action." A child's salvation depended entirely on a parent's ability to "make an evil natured but at least partly rational animal act against his nature and according to his reason." Had children been merely ignorant, nothing further would have been required, but because they were born evil as well, measures to restrain the passionate, impulsive elements of a child's nature became necessary. Parents were instructed to fill the child's mind with knowledge, to set a proper example and to apply discipline judiciously. Permitting "the lewd and wild courses" of childhood to go unchecked would deliver children directly to "Eternal Vengeance, the Unquenchable Flames of Hell."

Today most of us don't live in communities bound together by one set of unassailable moral principles, a common standard of conduct rooted in a consensual vision of good and evil. We don't have a single outlook on human nature as Puritan parents did to guide our actions as parents. In its place, modern parents confront multiple compelling and competing answers to the question of whether a child's behavior and character are malleable. Scientists debate this matter through controlled observations and elegant data analyses, and philosophers argue about the balance of passion and reason in human nature against the criterion of logical consistency. Mothers also explore the boundaries of this question, but not in impeccably reasoned letters to the editor in academic journals. Instead, we are more likely to be wrestling with this issue in our jeans or sweatpants, standing in front of a toddler in a high chair who has spit out, yet again, the mashed banana in rice cereal that the pediatrician authoritatively assured us, "*Every* baby learns to love."

We carry on dialogues on the playground, at parks and at work with other mothers about situations just like this one, situations that are cast in terms of the dichotomy between nature and nurture:

What do you think about the research that shows playing classical music for a baby in utero encourages synaptic development involved in mathematical problem solving?

Will my baby always wake up a couple times each night; is he just a light sleeper? or can I change his pattern by (shudder) ignoring him when he cries?

What kind of enrichment, if any, enhances motor development? cognitive development? language development?

Is it really true that environmental stimulation matters little after age three?

How do you teach a child responsibility? Does a star chart make sense? If I give my son or daughter a prize for doing something, how in the world will he or she learn to do things without the promise of a reward?

These are the debates about nature and nurture that mothers have, weighing choices that feel critical to the kind of individuals our children become. Unlike scientists and philosophers who can staunchly identify themselves with one position or the other, mothers usually find it very difficult, if not impossible, to do this. We swing back and forth between the position (nurture) that says, "Yes, this baby will be like any other baby, she will do what I want her to, she will learn to love bananas, I just have to exert the right kind of gentle pressure," and the opposite conclusion (nature), "Damn it. This child came into the world, and is going to leave it, hating bananas, no matter what I do!"

There was a time I thought that such inconstancy of outlook made me a less intelligent person somehow; not being able to stick to a single unwavering intellectual position made me a chaotic, flighty mother. In my early motherhood, I wanted to be informed, up-to-date on what the latest articles in the newspaper, issues of *Nature* and programs on *Nova* told me about my child and what I could and couldn't do for her. I paid attention to what was going on out there, kept track of the latest scientific advances because I wanted to be rational and enlightened about my decisions, able to offer a cogent, fact-filled explanation of my choices as a parent. In this matter, as in many others, my preparation as a psychologist did little to help me with these choices and questions.

I realized what I was looking for, like most young mothers, was some way to interpret what was going on with my child, a scheme that would help me to decide what to pay attention to and what I could ignore; what I had influence over and what I did not. I think this must be one reason the nature versus nurture paradigm has such a powerful hold on our imaginations. It seems to offer simplicity, certainty and security. The problem is that looking at children through the prism of nature-nurture can mean parents feel constrained to pick one side or the other, and in the process can inadvertently lose sight of their individual child's needs and complexity.

For a long time, the scientific methods used to study questions about the relative contribution of genes (nature) and environment (nurture) reinforced the idea that these two factors were opposing forces in a child's development. The traditional methods of analyzing research data imposed a relationship between nature and nurture in which genes and environment made separate and fixed contributions to a given trait, characteristic or developmental outcome. This was known as the additive model, and it assumed the following: genetic factors + environment = trait. Fortunately, contemporary research strategies and data analytic methods have allowed scientists to test more complex and sophisticated assumptions about the interplay of genetics and environment.

One of the most important of these more sophisticated assumptions is that a child's genetic inheritance manifests itself differently under different environmental conditions and experiences. This reformulation of the nature-nurture relationship is described in the research literature as the environment "mediating" or "moderating" the "expression" of genes. It suggests the relationship between genes and environment is interactive and dynamic rather than static and unvarying as implied in the older model. For example, all infants are genetically prepared to develop speech. However, the language that any given child eventually learns to speak depends on the language that he or she hears spoken. As another example, we know that the differences in children's height are best explained by the differences in the height of their biological parents.

Knowing this, we might conclude that environment has little to do with the height a child reaches in adulthood. Environmental "inputs" such as nutrition have been clearly shown however to moderate or influence height in a large population of individuals.

Contrary to some views currently popularized in the media, there is a good deal of evidence that parenting, regarded as an environmental factor, influences the behavioral expressions of a child's genetic endowment. One very good example comes from Grazyna Kochanska's research on the early development of conscience in children. In this research, conscience is defined as an awareness of "the moral goodness or blameworthiness of one's own conduct, intentions or character together with a feeling of obligation to do right or be good." It is measured by whether a child follows adult rules even when they have opportunities to break them.

The child's temperament, defined as a wide range of constitutionally based differences in children's reactions to the environment and in self-regulation, is considered a genetic characteristic. Kochanska used differences in temperament to identify two groups of children whose ages ranged from two to three. One group consisted of children who were timid and fearful when asked to explore new activities. The activities included jumping on a trampoline, putting a hand inside a large black box, and interacting with a clown. The second contrasting group was composed of fearless children who were receptive and eager to engage in those same activities. These two groups of children and their mothers were part of a longitudinal study and were evaluated at several points in time. The findings I summarize are on the children at age five.

Kochanska found that fearful children develop conscience earlier than fearless children. He speculated that the biologically rooted characteristic of fearfulness might enhance the rate that children internalize rules and norms for socially acceptable conduct. More interestingly, with temperamentally fearful children, the development of conscience was facilitated by a mother's use of disciplinary measures that deemphasized her use of power. These mothers avoided the use of angry comments, threats, restraint or physical enforcement when interacting with their more timid children. This emphasis on gentle forms of discipline was a sensitive and skillful adaptation of their disciplinary approach in response to their children's natural temperamental inclination.

In bold, fearless children, the development of strong internal control over conduct required a different kind of disciplinary approach. Rather than being able to work with a child's natural cautiousness to promote socially appropriate behavior, the mother of a fearless child capitalized instead upon the warm, positive relationship with her child to motivate him or her to do the right thing and make the morally correct choice. Mothers of fearless children who demonstrated a well-developed sense of conscience were warm and showed genuine enjoyment of their child, attunement to his or her emotional signals, and respect for the child's autonomy.

This research indicates that the style of a mother's discipline clearly influences how children with different temperaments begin to internalize rules to guide their behavior and control their impulses. It furthermore is a beautiful illustration of the newer understanding of how genes and environment interact. Although a mother cannot *alter* the genetic basis of her child's temperament, she can create different parenting environments around her child that optimize the child's development by sensitive accommodation of her child's temperament.

This more complex reality of the relationship between genes and parenting is not the usual image parents get from the popular media or the culture at large. The media generally supports the assumption that when something is "natural," it cannot be tampered with, and that it will resist any effort to modify its character. It is not surprising then for parents to invoke genes, gender or evolution as we try to account for something a child of ours has done or said, or failed to do or say. This frequently encountered notion of genes as impervious to what we do as parents means we can inadvertently fall into the habit of making allowance for actions that most children would benefit from being held accountable for. I have probably encountered this kind of thinking most in mothers' conversations about boys and about children parents consider gifted.

BOYS WILL BE BOYS. I remember watching helplessly as Emily at twenty-two months was bitten on the nose by a little boy about the same age. Although they didn't know each other, they had been quite happily playing side by side in the sandbox at our neighborhood park. It did not seem his action had been provoked in any way; there hadn't been a tussle over a shovel or pail, for example. He simply leaned over and bit her. As I daubed at the blood that afternoon and tried to calm my wailing child, his mother rushed up to me. I don't remember any longer exactly what she said. The gist of it was her son was "just being a little boy," and his biting my daughter was a Y-chromosome-driven gesture, caused by a force outside her control or ability to respond to constructively. "A phase," she told me her pediatrician had told her. It was "an unfortunate outlet for his excess activity."

After Emily stopped crying and the activity in the sandbox settled back to the usual scooping and dumping and patting of little hands, I realized how mad I was. I was mad about a lot of things: at myself for not having moved fast enough to protect her, at the pediatrician for that pat phrase, "just a phase," and at the mother for offering what had seemed like a confused and half-hearted apology, an assertion that nothing could be done or was required of her because her child happened to be a boy.

It took some time, but as I calmed down, I put myself in that other young mother's place. I remembered how shocked and dumbfounded she looked, and I began to wonder if she hadn't felt just as helpless and ill served by this notion about boys as I did. Even if the pediatrician hadn't meant to suggest that she shouldn't or couldn't do anything about her son's behavior, that message—that boys are, and maybe even should be, resistant to a mother's influence—is around us everywhere. Whether we are mothers of boys or not, it's seeped into our unconscious images of men, males and masculinity, and into our expectations about boys.

I started to think that because she was the mother of a boy and I was the mother of a girl we had played out the opposite sides of the issue about boys and aggression. To protect her son, and to keep me from thinking she was a bad mother or her son was a bad boy, she had simply said the first thing that popped into her mind. It happened to be one of those easy, sound-bite phrases, plucked off the cultural airwaves, that maybe she didn't really believe, but found herself saying anyway because she had heard it so many times and in so many ways. And even though I know the research literature makes clear that boys are more likely than girls to be physically aggressive, this knowledge didn't keep me from wanting someone (not just the Y chromosome) to be held accountable for what had happened.

I'd like to believe that if we had been friends, not strangers, we would have talked about all of this. We would have commiserated about how much harder raising a son can feel to women, especially those who abhor aggression in any form, sorting though the various positions on the nature of boys—their rough and tumble play, their "hyper" activity and their aggressive behavior. I'm sorry to say we didn't have that conversation. And I'm especially sorry to say that other young mother didn't return to sit serenely on the bench near the sandbox with the rest of us, but packed her child and all his playthings into the stroller and without saying good-bye fled from the park as if pursued by a pack of wild dogs.

It isn't easy to have a clear fix on all the ideas there are about boys and what everyone says is their propensity to act in and on the world in more physical and unrestrained ways, ways we are told are different from those of girls and women. Almost every one of my friends with a son or two describes the ways their boys typically behave as more "wild," "unresponsive," "hyper" or "physical" when compared to their daughters or girls they know well. They speak about their sons as being more naturally aggressive, and as quite young children, as having been more resistant or impervious to their efforts to correct their behavior.

All of us can think of kindergarten classrooms where certain boys are always the students wandering around the class, sitting outside the group, wrestling with another boy on the periphery of the reading circle, forgetting to raise a hand, having a hard time waiting their turn and shouting answers out. Boys have a harder time than girls adjusting their activity level to requirements of a physically contained situation such as a classroom. It is as though the high-energy, impulsive nature of their behavior is harder to rein in and get under control.

It is interesting to note that a good deal of research evidence suggests that boys aren't in an absolute sense more active than girls. This research indicates that from birth to age two, any differences in activity level between boys and girls are quite small. And there aren't any differences, at any age, when boys and girls play alone. Rather, boys are more physically active when they are playing with other boys and playing in groups of boys. In other words, the nature of boys' activity level is highly context dependent.

It is true that when boys and girls are observed in natural environments of playgroups and classrooms, on average, boys are more physically aggressive than girls are. Aggression is taken to be "behavior which hurts or appears intended to do so." This sex difference in physical aggression is observed in groups of children as young as three and continues to characterize boys' and girls' interpersonal relationships through adolescence. The qualification, "on average," is a very important one, however. Just as my friend Janet discovered with her daughter Hannah, not every girl is "sugar and spice and everything nice," many boys are quiet, self-contained, and rarely, if ever, retaliate physically against another child. In other words, not every boy is more aggressive than every girl; but in any given group of children, the chances are that the children who *are* the most physically aggressive will be boys.

Just as boys' activity level is highly context dependent, so is their aggressive behavior highly context dependent. Boys are more likely to engage in physically aggressive actions when they are playing with other boys, and when they perceive the actions of playmates as a threat to their status in the group. Interestingly, when boys play with girls, they are less physically aggressive, and when girls play with boys, they become more aggressive. It appears then that male aggression is more likely to occur in conjunction with specific situational cues, including interaction with other boys.

Over the course of development most boys and girls learn to inhibit aggressive impulses. However, some researchers argue that differences in the rates of neurological maturation contribute to the observed difference in boys' and girls' physical aggression. Girls may be more developmentally able to inhibit physical aggression and to learn socially acceptable methods of resolving conflict. Boys as a group may be slower to develop the neurodevelopmental underpinnings that support the inhibition of aggressive impulses and the acquisition of socially appropriate interpersonal skills. Researchers note for instance that boys with longstanding histories of physical aggression differ from nonaggressive boys in that they have more poorly developed cognitive processes known as the "executive functions" or "control functions." These functions are reflected in behaviors such as the ability to learn contingency rules, to use feedback to adjust behavior, to inhibit a set of reactions and to anticipate future events in order to regulate behavior.

Studies by Nikki Crick and her colleagues have challenged the popular conception that boys are more aggressive than girls, and introduced the concept of "relational aggression" to address nonphysical forms of aggression. Crick's work has clarified that girls are not less aggressive than boys, but that they express aggression interpersonally rather than physically. She defines relational aggression as "behaviors that harm others through damage (or the threat of damage) to relationships or feelings of acceptance, friendship or group inclusion."

Most research on relational aggression has focused on children in middle childhood, that is on children between the ages of nine and twelve, but there are some studies on children from three to five years of age. During both the preschool and middle school years, when compared to boys, girls are more likely to be relationally aggressive and less physically aggressive. In contrast to this, boys are more likely to be physically and less relationally aggressive than girls. By enlarging our notion of aggressive behavior to include nonphysical forms of aggression, the popular conception of boys as more aggressive than girls is not supported. Instead, very interesting questions are raised about the biological, familial and social factors that might account for this gender divergence.

GENIUS AT WORK. DO NOT DISTURB. Unlike the parent who believes certain children are or should be naturally impervious to outside influence, there are parents who assume certain children must be protected from external influence. These parents believe a child's nature should be allowed expression without being hampered by the requirements of the outside world. They interpret external expectations and structure merely as impediments to their child's development, believing they promote undesirable qualities and outcomes such as conformity and the loss of uniqueness. As a consequence, parents with this viewpoint can inadvertently overlook a child's real need for parents to impose guidance and to set limits.

Nathan and Cynthia were parents like this. From the time their youngest child, Cameron, was able to walk, all of his mischievous behavior, the kind every child experiments with, was looked upon as "charming," "clever" or "ingenious." His antics were applauded and described as signs that he was truly a unique and extraordinarily gifted child. His parents resisted the advice of friends and families, no matter how mildly or kindly put, about how they might help Cam with what they began to call his "strong-willed" nature, although they routinely asked for it. They rejected any suggestion that Cam's mischievous activities were really questions that every child asks of his parent, even if they are asking through their behavior and not in words: "Are you looking at me? Do you care? Do you care enough to keep me safe and close to you? Do you care enough to say 'no' to me?

At two years of age, Cam's temper tantrums were massive and protracted. When a tantrum hit, Nathan and Cynthia took turns talking to him, attempting to reason with their son, confident that if he understood the importance of "doing the right thing," he would because he wanted to. They could not tolerate feeling that they were "coercive" parents. The notion that unlimited, unrestrained self-expression could be frightening and overwhelming to a toddler was foreign to Nathan and

Cynthia's view of their child, and probably more important, to their view of themselves as parents. More than
once, I watched a temper tantrum that ended only when
Cam had exhausted himself. Cynthia, also exhausted,
would smile wanly and explain once more that he was
"just overtired."

Troubles began when Cam started school and he had to
leave the protected cocoon of his immediate family and
their interpretation of his behavior. After an exhaustive
search for the right nursery school and an initial phase of
being completely enthralled with their choice, Cynthia
began describing the school's schedule as rigid and the
teachers as lacking warmth and a real understanding of
her son. She did not remove Cam from the school, but
regularly expressed her dissatisfaction to close friends. It
came as no surprise to those who knew this family well
that the transition to kindergarten was difficult, and
when Cam started the first grade he began to complain of
headaches and stomachaches every morning. Once he got
to school, he would frequently end up in the nurse's office
asking to make a call to his mother.

Cynthia was convinced Cam's reactions indicated he
was insufficiently challenged by the academic work. She
believed his refusal to go to school was a natural, completely understandable and acceptable reaction to the
school's inability to be responsive to her child's unusual
gifts and sensitive temperament. Believing his physical
complaints expressed his thwarted brilliance and creativ-
ity, she began to disparage the school and look for more

specialized school settings. With each passing year, Cynthia and Nathan became more firmly entrenched in their view of their child's fragility and unique needs. By the time Cam was a teenager, he had begun to express his need for limits and discipline more dramatically, becoming aggressive toward others and engaging in minor antisocial acts such a shoplifting and truancy from school.

————

Finding the right balance of restriction and autonomy when setting and enforcing expectations for a child is one of the greatest ongoing challenges parents face. Most parents have a characteristic way of dealing with this challenge, something socialization researchers call a "parenting style." Any given parent's approach to this issue can usually be described in one of four ways: authoritative, authoritarian, permissive or uninvolved. Authoritative parenting combines high demands for maturity with warmth and responsiveness to the needs and demands of the child. Authoritarian parents impose high expectations and rigid disciplinary practices and are not terribly responsive or warm. Uninvolved parents neither require much from their children in terms of involvement with the family or expectations for mature behavior nor demonstrate responsiveness and warmth. Permissive parents are very responsive, but impose few demands for maturity. Of these four types of parenting, authoritative parenting is the parenting style most consistently associated with positive developmental outcomes in children.

I will say with some ambivalence that being a parent

with "high demands" comes a little too easily to me. This is probably because I haven't completely exorcised the imprint of the battle my Christian missionary grandfather waged against the devil in Japan and that he waged at home as a father for the souls of his children. Most of my friends worry about the modern evils which surround our children: guns, drugs, precocious and unprotected sex, car accidents, murder, rape, pornographic television, movies and chat rooms. I am old-fashioned in that I am a parent who is sometimes gripped not by the prospect of the evils that might assault my children from the outside, but about those that might tempt them from within.

My maternal grandfather believed, as the Puritans did, that no aspect of human behavior was outside the reign of reason: "[M]an does nothing by compulsion, 'nor by the force of instinct,' but by rational determination, by intellectual comprehension, even when he comprehends imperfectly." Most afternoons during my childhood he sat at one end of the long dining room table and patiently copied out onto translucent white paper long passages written by German philosopher Immanuel Kant, a philosopher whose views corresponded with his own.

Naturally left-handed, he was forced as a student to use his right hand instead. Passionate about becoming a doctor, a late-detected heart murmur forced his withdrawal from medical school. A second-born son at a time when patrimony was the social and legal custom, he left his family to make a life in America. I think that my grandfather must have yearned to escape from a destiny defined

by caprice and convention, and in its stead adopted a phi-
losophy that valorized personal agency and effort.

His aspirations for his three oldest children reflected
the optimism about human potential he embraced in his
new life in America. His oldest daughter was to become a
doctor, his first-born son, an engineer, and my mother, a
pharmacist, for the most part, all occupational choices
quite blind to the interests and talents of his children. He
shared the first American behaviorist John Watson's faith
in the infinite malleability of humans: "Give me a dozen
healthy infants, well-formed, and my own specified world
to bring them up in and I'll guarantee to take any one at
random and train him to become any type of specialist I
might select—doctor, lawyer, artist, merchant-chief and
yes, even beggar-man and thief, regardless of his talents,
penchants, tendencies, abilities, vocation, and race of his
ancestors."

An outspoken advocate of scientific child rearing during the 1920s and 1930s, Watson authored not only the
influential guide *The Psychological Care of Infant and
Child,* in which this statement appeared, but also numer-
ous articles aimed at mothers that appeared regularly in
Collier's and *Harper's.* For me, this outlook is packaged in
an evangelist's hellfire and brimstone vision of the proper
life, but it need not be. This conviction that children can
become whoever and whatever their (or our) hearts desire
is democratic in its spirit. Americans admire children
who overcome the insurmountable to become heroic; and

admire the parents who believe in them, coach, coax and form them into individuals of noteworthy talent and character.

I knew something of the hardship my mother and her older sister and brother suffered because they did not fulfill my grandfather's vision of who and what they could make of themselves. There were hints, never details, about the emotional distress of loving an impassioned parent who lacks a sense of proportion in this ancient debate between nature and nurture. I would love to say that out of sympathy for my mother and her siblings, I became the moderate parent that my grandfather was not. That my position on the nature-nurture issue was a temperate one, acknowledging that the person a child becomes is a complex interaction of what a child arrives with at birth and life experiences. But instead it is my grandfather's deep-seated belief that if you just try hard enough anything is possible that expresses itself first.

———

One afternoon when Rachel was either three or four, she had a friend over to play. I overhead them arguing, and I was sure the conflict had erupted because at three and four Rachel liked to be in charge. She needed to be first, the first child at the classroom door in the morning, the first to finish a race, the fastest, the quickest. Most everyone responded to her as the enlivening spirit of our little clan. They admired her independent mindedness and saw it as a path toward health, sturdiness and success. On the other hand, I always worried about the repercussions of her re-lentless push toward recognition, her need to have her ideas prevail. She heard the words "sharing," "cooperate" and "being a good friend" a lot, probably too much and too soon for such a tiny person. All because I feared she would fall from grace: from the grace of others, from the grace of the mothers of her playmates, and who knows, maybe even from the grace of God, too. My fear that she would be my fallen angel drove me, in my quietly deter-mined way, to create what I realize must have been too large a pressure on her tender soul.

That afternoon I overheard Rachel apologize to her playmate after a stormy exchange, each having been furi-ous and immovable, "I am trying my hardest to be "Friendly" and "Cooperative," BUT I JUST CAN'T HELP MYSELF!" I felt awful. I knew her friend had not driven her to this outburst. I had. Me and the enduring power of the idea that if you just try hard enough, you can do any-thing.

———

My mother gave up studying chemistry, graduated from college, grew to young womanhood and became a mother harboring the belief that, at seventeen, she had not tried hard enough. She never questioned my grandfather's faith in the power of nurture or the emotional toll that it had extracted, but questioned herself instead. She was never free to celebrate the gifts and talents she had been en-dowed with naturally, and I suspect died believing she had been a disappointment to her father.

_____

The psychologist who consulted me about his patient Tyler asked to talk with me again after a few months. He asked to meet because Tyler had begun to refuse to take his medicine. Like a prisoner of war, he had begun to pocket the suspect substance in his cheek, only to spit it out when he was safely out of his mother's watchful eye. He did this, even though he said the medicine helped him, because he was determined to win his father's approval and respect, to be a shining example of manly self-control. He wanted to be someone his dad was proud of. Tyler's father claimed he was guiltless in his son's subterfuge. His proof was that he had never once told him not to take his medicine. He said that that was Tyler's choice, and he was proud of him for making it.

Since learning Puritan parents were urged to consider a child's disposition in order to apply educational measures judiciously, I have had to reconsider my grandfather's fervor and sense of righteousness in his guidance of his children. Maybe judiciousness is a virtue harder to achieve without community elders to temper and guide the overzealous parent, or in an era where the time to learn about one's child well enough to know what is judicious and what is excessive is harder to find.

I've achieved a state of peaceful cohabitation with the residue of my grandfather's moralistic fervor. It hasn't gone away. I've just learned that I need to watch myself so it doesn't intrude on my efforts to be a judicious parent. But, of course, it still does from time to time. It happens when I am under too much pressure from other places in my life, when the complexity and intractability of a problem at work makes me want to make the complexity of my children just disappear. When I can't control other things that are important to me, I grasp at the illusion that by sheer force of a parent's personality and desire, children will be, and do, what is required of them.

For parents raised with the opposing viewpoint, that nature should be allowed to run its course, without interference, there are hazards of a different sort: expecting too little from our children, missing opportunities to provide guidance and direction, saying no. I do not know that tale from the inside, but I see it is merely the other point to which the pendulum swings from the position that I inhabit.

The wisest mothers I know seem to arrive at a different view of human nature, one that gently dismantles the nature-nurture paradigm. They seem not to assume that an opposition exists between nature and nurture, or that the relationship to their children is fixed and unchanging. They seem to assume fluidity of a child's character and see fewer contradictions, or are untroubled by the ones they do see. They seem perpetually open and accepting of whatever happens with their children, willing to revisit and refine their notion of who this person is as he or she changes and grows. And they seem to have found ways to suspend the need for certainty in their understanding of their children, and are able to turn a blind eye to what other people are doing with, or for, their children. They wait and watch, like a gardener who has scattered seed of unknown origin waits for signs to tell her whether she will have beans or a pumpkin come the summer.

When I've asked these mothers about this difference in their outlook, they laugh and tell me their children "grew them up," or they laugh and say they did what worked for their children. They remind me of the head nurse I worked with early in my training who took in all the passionately argued statements from her young staff about what made the most sense in the discharge planning for a highly asthmatic, steroid-dependent boy named Andrew. Then without resorting to scolding or shaming, she pointed out that every single one of our arguments was about what would be convenient or inconvenient to us, and reminded us that the way to make our decisions was to "keep our eyes on the child."

———

I used to play a game as a child that I see every once in a while when I am cruising the mall with my girls. I remember that playing it felt a lot like what these mothers tell me. I don't remember what it is called, but I do remember it is a game of skill. You play it alone, and not against any one else. It consists of a pair of metal rods hinged together on one end of an oblong wooden board. You hold the free end of the rods, one in each hand, and a metal ball about the size of a large marble rests on top of them.

The object of the game is to get the ball to move away from you, up the slightly inclined rods. It is tougher than it looks and requires a lot of time to figure out how to make it work for you. Favoring one rod over the other never works, the ball falls with a very loud "thunk" every single time if you do. If you are stubborn, and don't adjust your approach, don't let yourself experiment with different relationships between the rods, you'll keep hearing that "thunk." Guaranteed.

I asked someone who knows about this sort of thing, about the physics of such gravity-defying movements, and she told me the forward motion was momentum created by the transfer of energy. There is beauty and poetry in my friend's explanation. The image of neat, efficient energy units moving steadily through the rods and into the marble just like those arrows from the physics filmstrips Mr. Walker used to show to our class. But I preferred to look at the steady progress of that shiny orb across the empty spaces as a kind of magic, ignoring the study that went into making it happen. Progressing up the ramp all on its own, under its own steam. I like to feel that same sense of mystery about my children, that they are sprouting up and moving ahead because of irresistible and predestined forces. That this all happens by magic. The reality is that such magic doesn't happen without work; the trick is to make the work steady and invisible, the backdrop, not the foreground. It keeps the mystery alive.

I think it is this sense of wonder that my wise mother friends have, a willingness to be surprised and delighted. They make room for different aspects of a child, even those that contradict what they thought before. I don't know if my grandfather could have been such a parent. I don't know if it was in his disposition to offer this delicate, yet paradoxically rock solid balance of humility and steady receptivity to a child's evolution. But since I can't believe any longer, no matter how much I have loved him, that this is determined by disposition alone, I have looked around for help to achieve what my wise mother friends have learned.

What I found was this quotation from Annie Dillard's *Holy the Firm.* I have it tacked onto my pencil holder above my desk. I think my grandfather would have been pleased that I find inspiration from another seeker of God, even if it is not from the holy scripture that my inspiration comes: "And now outside the window, deep on the horizon, a new thing appears, as if we needed a new thing. It is a new land blue beyond islands, hitherto hidden by haze and now revealed, . . . I check my chart, my amateur penciled sketch of the skyline . . . Yes, this land is new, this spread blue spark beyond yesterday's new wrinkled line . . . How long can this go on? But let us by all means extend the scope of our charts."

INDEPENDENCE AND
DEPENDENCE

Late one Sunday morning in February several years ago, I sat at a large, rough-hewn kitchen table in an old New England farmhouse listening to a story about a mother, her child and the high value our culture places on independence. I had driven with my husband and girls to Putney, Vermont with a trunkful of balloons to celebrate the forty-something birthday of an old friend. After years of such gatherings I knew almost all the guests. One of the people I hadn't met before was Molly. She was close to forty, an art curator, and the mother of a son not quite two. We spent a bit of time together after breakfast that Sunday morning because we had drawn the short lots to become the designated dishwashers. While everyone else went sledding, we washed and dried mugs, glasses, plates and silverware for twenty, and powered our way through a sinkful of pots and pans. Finishing the last skillet, we settled into a conversation over fresh coffee, enjoying the peace and quiet of the empty house.

Whatever else being a child psychologist has meant, I can safely say it hasn't been much of a social asset. Most of the time when I tell someone what I do, a startled, deer-caught-in-the-headlights look flashes across her face. I have concluded after years of watching this happen that the listener is wondering whether my training has so finely tuned my powers of perception that I can read their minds. That look is typically followed either by the question, "And what age are the children you work with?" or the statement, "It must be very satisfying work." Molly had a different reaction. She said neither, but exclaimed, "Really! How wonderful! I've always wanted to ask someone about something that happened when I was young. Would you mind me telling you about it? It's a classic first day of school story." I said I'd be happy to listen, and she proceeded to tell me her story.

———

Molly grew up in a suburb of Minneapolis where all the children went to school by bus. When the big day arrived for Molly to go off to kindergarten, she and her mother waited on that first Monday morning at the designated corner with every other five-year-old child and his or her mother from their neighborhood. They stood last in the line, watching the other children peck their mothers on the cheek, clamber up the steps and into the bus. But when Molly's turn came to do the same, she refused and would not let go of her mother's hand. She remembered her mother speaking gently and patiently, attempting to coax her to board the bus, but to no avail. Molly wouldn't budge. The lineup of cars behind the bus was growing longer and her mother soon waved the bus along, telling the driver she would take Molly to school herself that morning.

On the drive to school, Molly's mother talked in the most soothing, reassuring tones possible about what fun Molly would have, what a big girl she was now, and reminding her about how much they had looked forward to this first day of kindergarten. When they got there, her mother didn't park and walk her to her classroom as Molly had expected. She drove to the front entrance of the school and told Molly it was time for her to go and that she mustn't be late. Molly managed to get the car door open, but at the last moment, lunged toward her mother and wrapped her arms around her neck, tears sliding slowly down her face. Her mother's body tensed, and in a voice unfamiliar to Molly, tersely called out to a passing teacher, "Would you kindly take her from me, please." The teacher did, cheerily encouraging Molly to wave good-bye to her mother as the car turned and drove away.

I learned this memory was fresh in Molly's mind because she had spoken to her mother a few months earlier hoping to ease the confusion and hurt she still felt. She thought she had done a very good job of bringing up her feelings from that morning without anger or accusation, yet was disappointed by her mother's defensiveness. What she had said to Molly was, "I thought if I gave in to you, there would be no end to it. I did what I thought was best for you. I had no other choice."

Molly looked thoughtful. She told me that as a five-year-old she could be "more than a little melodramatic," and said she knew exactly what her mother had meant by "there would be no end to it." But she remembered as a child having been disturbed by the feeling that something had happened to turn her kind, patient mother into "a witch" who refused to hug and comfort her, but had instead coolly tossed her out into the world. Molly sat absorbed in her own thoughts for a long time, and then with fresh feeling asked, "Would it really have been so hard for her to let me cling just a little longer? I was only a baby."

————

I wasn't sure how Molly would react to the answer that came to mind, but I liked her. She seemed down to earth and very straightforward. I decided it didn't make any sense to be the neutral professional, that I should just be honest with her. So I said, "This probably isn't the answer you were hoping to hear, but yes, I do think it would have been hard. It would have been very hard. After all, what mother in America doesn't feel she must do her absolute utmost to raise children others see as independent and self-reliant?"

————

The ideal that Molly's mother was grappling with, the ideal of the clear-sighted, inner-directed citizen, able to withstand external pressure toward conformity has a long history in American culture. In fact, this aspect of our national character was evident to Alexis de Tocqueville, the eminent French social philosopher, not long after the American Revolution. He came to America to observe political life in a society founded on the principle of human equality. To his surprise, he found not egalitarianism, but individualism; the belief in the dignity of the individual and in one's right to think and speak freely was our most cherished value as Americans.

This notion of the independent-minded individual was reiterated sixty years later by the influential American educational philosopher John Dewey as the moral foundation of a democracy. In 1887 he wrote, "The society of which the child is to be a member, is in the United States, a democratic and progressive society. The child must be educated for leadership as well as for obedience. He must have power of self-direction and power of directing others, powers of administration, ability to assume positions of responsibility."

For most of our nation's history, men like John Dewey were addressing fathers, not mothers, when they spoke about the personal attributes of the ideal American citizen. As was true for most of recorded history, men, not women, were entrusted with the religious and moral upbringing of children.

This convention followed from the premise that men are rational and women are not. Parental objectivity and detachment were considered absolutely necessary to oversee a child's education adequately. Men, unlike women, were not subject to sentimentality or excess emotion that would threaten a reasoned perspective on a child's rearing. According to historian John Demos, this assumption was commonly accepted by Puritan men and women alike: "Carried to and fro by their inordinate affection and lacking the 'compass' of sound reason, women could hardly provide the vigilant supervision all children needed."

For Puritan parents, the proper rearing of a child was a responsibility of enormous consequence. In marked contrast to our modern child-rearing values, "There was no question of developing the child's personality, of drawing out or nourishing any desirable inherent qualities which he might possess, for no child could by nature possess any desirable qualities. He had to receive all good from outside himself, from education—and ultimately from the Holy Spirit."

A child's salvation and personal communication with God depended entirely on how well the parent "educated" him or her. A cornerstone of that education was the earliest possible training to be self-reliant. In keeping with this goal, Puritan parents, for example, abandoned the centuries old custom of infants and young children sleeping with their mothers and fathers. In its place they introduced the custom of moving infants into an unshared bed as soon as possible. By instituting this new practice, they believed they were protecting the souls of their infant children. Rather than an expression of coldheartedness, it represented an act of parental love and Christian piety.

This cultural assumption of men's superiority to women in the task of raising children began a slow process of transformation as New England underwent its economic evolution from an agrarian to an industrial economy. For centuries the work of men and women was carried out at home. It was a joint domestic enterprise with fathers and mothers in close physical proximity to children and each other.

The Industrial Revolution radically altered this arrangement. Men worked for a paid wage outside the home and women worked within the domestic sphere of home, and for the first time created separate spheres of labor, male and female. As fathers increasingly spent their working hours physically absent from home, wife and children, they were less able to fulfill their social role as the parent primarily responsible for guiding and rearing the children. This responsibility gradually fell to mothers. However, this shift occurred without revision of the assumption that women were naturally ill suited to the task. In the eyes of the culture, they remained poor substitutes for father and his greater natural capacity for rational thought.

The cultural response to the dilemma of father's absence was the emergence of secular authorities on matters of child development. These authorities, usually male, replaced the religious authorities of previous generations, and emphasized to mothers the necessity of adopting child-rearing measures that would hold the undesirable "female" attributes of sentimentality and irrationality in check.

The rational approach to child rearing popularized by the first behaviorists during the 1920s and 1930s is an example of such an approach. Mothers were advised to care for their babies according to a strict and rigid schedule. These were believed to serve as necessary restraint against maternal sentimentality and tenderheartedness. Feeding, diapering, cradling and especially attention to crying were rigidly scheduled events. Deviation from the timetable carried the risk of ill-preparing one's child for the rigors of adult self-sufficiency. In a stern voice representative of the era, John Watson warned mothers not to yield to their more softhearted urges: "When you are tempted to pet your child remember that mother love is a dangerous instrument. An instrument which may inflict a never healing wound, a wound which may make infancy unhappy, adolescence a nightmare, an instrument which may wreck your adult son or daughter's vocational future and their chances for marital happiness."

The notion that a mother's involvement with her children threatened their emotional and social adjustment, particularly in the case of boys, became more prominent in the years immediately preceding World War II. One of the pioneering theorists in the field of family therapy, Olga Silverstein, describes her first encounters with the deeply rooted conviction that a mother's protective instinct, especially a mother's instinct toward a son, was always a threat to his independence, and must therefore be reined in and suppressed.

Silverstein gave birth to her first child, Michael, in the

early years of World War II when her husband was away at war. She tells us it was not unusual for women to give birth to their first babies during these years in spite of the wartime uncertainty of their spouse's safe return.

One day when Michael was about a year old and I was feeling particularly nervous—we were all nervous all the time during the war years—I took him to a pediatrician and explained that I had come because my baby seemed "tense." I think now that I was simply looking for a man to tell me Michael was fine, as indeed he was. The doctor looked at me sternly and told me I was hovering too much. "Get off the boy's back," he said. Which was the beginning of what I now see as the long process of pulling back and monitoring myself.

A few months later, not along after Michael started to walk, I took him to a fancy specialist, because he was so pigeon-toed he was tripping over his own feet and I thought maybe he needed some kind of corrective shoes. This man was even sterner. "What this boy needs," he said, while shaking his finger at me, "is a little judicious neglect." . . . Two years after, {again} in response to my concern about Michael appearing "tense," our pediatrician suggested that he needed his independence. "Send him out by himself," he advised. "By himself?" I repeated, in some surprise. He was only three and a half, and we were at the time living in the Bronx, in a pleasant enough but busy, populous, urban neighborhood. "Yes, you have to let him go. Stop protecting him all the time." So of course I did try to allow him to be more independent. In retrospect I would describe Michael as intense, rather than tense. His being a very intelligent child, acutely aware of and responsive to his environment, led naturally to his taking everything to heart. He didn't need to be off on his own; he needed someone to talk to about his many concerns— one of which, surely, was that he had just met his father, newly returned from World War II, for the first time.

Much like my new friend Molly's mother, Silverstein was caught in a conflict between her intuitive understanding that her child needed something from her and the cultural message that a mother's natural feeling, or understanding, for her child was not important or worth paying attention to. Rather it had to be held in check, especially if it appeared to encourage the child's dependence rather than autonomy and self-sufficiency.

Happily for many mothers of the 1950s, the idea that a mother's instinct could not be trusted was countered in the book *Dr. Spock's Baby and Child Care.* Written by pediatrician Benjamin Spock this formidable compendium offered wise and cheering counsel about the worries all new parents experience, blending sound medical advice with the kind, supportive presence of a loving family friend. The doctor assured new mothers that it would be all right for them to abandon the highly regimented, self-restricting childrearing approach of the two previous decades, and by implication, and most important, the prohibition against maternal feeling and responsiveness. Women reading the first edition were greeted with this encouragement on the very first page:

TRUST YOURSELF. You know more than you think you do. Soon you're going to have a baby. Maybe you have one already. You're happy and excited, but if you haven't had much experience, you wonder whether you are going to know how to do a good job. . . . Don't take too seriously all that the neighbors say. Don't be overawed by what the experts say. Don't be afraid to trust your own common sense. Bringing up your child won't be a complicated job if you take it easy, trust your own instincts, and follow the directions that your doctor gives you.

Following Spock, the child development experts of the next three decades, the years from the 1950s through the 1970s, no longer portrayed women as constitutionally ill suited to the tasks and responsibilities of parenthood. Nor did they imply that maternal instinct or intuition was inimical to a child's development and successful life adjustment. They did, however, continue to suggest to modern mothers, in a message not too dissimilar from that fashioned for Puritan mothers, that good mothering required self-restraint. Not as a response to something bad and corrupting in themselves, but in response to something instinctive and natural in a child, namely every child's desire to be separate and independent from the mother. Psychoanalyst Louise Kaplan wrote, "Nobody has to tell a baby when to begin to separate. . . . a human baby flourishes only when he can gratify his urge to uproot and get moving."

This characterization of autonomy-seeking as the natural, spontaneous desire of every child subtly recast the measure of the good mother from her ability to resist coddling a child to her ability to respect, and yield to, a child's need for separation and independent exploration. In this view, emotional self-sufficiency, independence and separation are developmental inevitabilities in the life of every baby. From the time he or she can walk, every boy and girl will begin to depend only intermittently upon the mother, these reunions being predictable, time-limited phases in development. The mother's actual presence becomes less and less necessary as the child gradually builds a storehouse of memories of the kind of care received. These memories become a source of emotional support and refreshment turned to at times of stress, memories that will enable the young child to rely more fully on him or herself and to find pleasure in being apart from mother.

Most pediatricians and child development experts have continued to argue that a child's striving for independence is a biologically inherent desire that parents cannot alter. For instance, T. Berry Brazelton states: "The drive for the child to become independent is a force that is built into the maturation process. It first appears when babies stand up at about the age of five months. They brighten and giggle as if saying, "This is it! This is what I've been waiting for!"

In a slightly different vein, Penelope Leach cautions that parents' attempts to tamper with this drive will not only be at some cost to their child, but to their relationship to him or her, as well: "If you expect your toddler to remain what he was—a comparatively compliant baby— you will be wrong; he will have to clash with you directly. He needs your love and approval, but his desire to grow up will not allow him to accept them at the price of too much dependence."

Not every mother takes these prescriptions to heart, of course. Some cultural groups don't place as high a value on independence in children as our middle-class American one, and mothers like my black friend Justine or my Puerto Rican friend Amalia seem less absorbed by this issue. I think I was a pretty typical young mother in having to struggle some to figure out exactly what I thought about this imperative to raise an independent child. I remember many times privately debating just how I was supposed to translate this principle into concrete terms that would help with the kind of decisions I faced, like Emily's refusal to budge from her little pink seat and going limp each time I tried to pick her up. What exactly was I seeing when she frantically stretched her arms out over the bars of her crib, crying at three in the morning? Was this dependence that needed to be quashed immediately or could I yield to what felt like real fear, and not just this once, but maybe a lot? Could I do this and not wreck her for life?

I asked myself lots of questions like this. Where was the line between too much closeness and the behaviors that would trumpet my child's independence and self-sufficiency? If I weaned her late, would she miss out on some crucial opportunity to experience herself as separate and autonomous and healthy? If I waited until she was four to enroll her in nursery school, not three as is the norm, or not at all, would she be inappropriately tied to me? Would she be held back in some small way, the consequences unknown until she went off to college? Would she grow up to be an independent person?

———

The research of feminist scholars in psychology such as Jean Baker Miller, Carol Gilligan, Judith Jordan and others has offered an alternate view of the meaning and value of independence and dependence in our culture. This collective body of scholarship has brought into clearer relief the essential place of attachment, relationship and intimacy in human growth and development. Until their work was undertaken, theories of psychological development were based primarily on the study of men and not women. As a consequence, our conceptions of healthy development tended to emphasize attributes such as autonomy, emotional containment, interpersonal competition and individual achievement as markers of psychological health. These are qualities understood to be especially adaptive in male contexts. However, when the psychological experience of women was also explored, attributes such as empathy and contextual reasoning were highlighted. When we regard these traits not as inherently female, but as human capacities, we are able to ask important questions about the social conditions that support, as well as suppress, them.

In spite of revisionist ideas and research, the image of the independent child as the child esteemed above all others remains a cornerstone of our understanding of children and of ourselves as mothers. It is the gold standard, the litmus test of whether a child is a good and admirable child and whether a mother is a good mother. On the flip side, there is dependence and the assumption that too great a need for mother inevitably indicates development gone awry.

The problem with this duality is that there is no middle ground. There is no recognition of the countless times in a child's life that are in-between, a little of both or one in some situations and its opposite in others. There is scant allowance for a mother's hard-nosed appraisal of a child as "shy" or "easily frightened" or "uncomfortable" with rough and tumble play that does not carry the risk of the silently critical appraisal of others. In a worldview that insists intellect and rationality are separate from feeling and sentiment, there is no such thing as a mother's reasoned tenderness.

At one time I saw my conflict about the duality of independence and dependence as an idiosyncratic one, one that arose uniquely because of my Japanese-American upbringing. It is not the failure to separate from others that constitutes the Japanese concept of existential terror, but the failure to establish and sustain relationships, to be excluded from the circle of intimate relationships. There is an ongoing concern with belonging, interdependence, empathy and reciprocity. In Japan, the expression "leaving home" is reserved for the rare event of a son severing his ties to the ordinary world to enter the monastic life. In America, "to leave home" is the destiny of every child.

Babies in Japan are born into a Shinto and Buddhist culture that views the natural world and the human world as continuous, in which the distinctions between good and evil, human and nonhuman, animate and inanimate, are not drawn as sharply as in the West. According to Shinto and Buddhist belief, babies are heavenly gifts from the gods who must be treated with leniency if they are to be persuaded to remain on earth. They are born in a state of disconnection from others, without an a priori attachment to a family—not, as in Western cosmology, dependent from the outset upon the mother. Transforming this state of disconnection to one of deep, enduring attachment is necessary if the baby is to become a member of its family and, more important, find a place in the earthly social order.

This is a task of enormous consequence, and it is the mother's first responsibility to the child. Fulfilling it depends on her ability to convince the baby that she is an individual worthy of its trust. She does so by coaxing the child to rely on her, continuously directing the child's attention inward toward the calm comfort of their relationship rather than to the dizzying rush of sights and sounds of the world outside. She is an unremitting physical presence during waking and sleeping—holding, carrying and rocking, allowing the baby's body to rest against hers. "Molded" in this way to one another, Japanese mothers and babies gave early Western anthropologists the impression of their being fused. Through her sensitivity to the nuances of the baby's state of being, the mother creates over and over, many times each day, a sense of well-being that the baby comes to associate with close mutual dependence. She fosters a sense of identity that will allow this child eventually to embody, not the Western notion of a distinct, separate, autonomous self, but the Japanese definition of self: *jibun,* meaning "one's share of the life space."

———

Over the years I've concluded that mine was in fact not a unique dilemma after all. I might have felt the tug between closeness and separateness in a different way because of my cultural heritage, but it is a struggle most mothers in middle-class America have. Our culture makes it difficult to trust our feelings, to give in to that pull toward supporting our children's dependence and see it as valuable, natural and good for children. Most mothers know intuitively that what we want for our children is to be independent without having to deny attachment, independent without having to deny needing others, independent without emotional isolation and a loss of feeling for other people, or forgoing the satisfaction that comes from belonging to a community. Yet most of us find we must work hard to resist the cultural message that "denial of the need of the other" is the one and only route to independence.

In American society, the weight of this expectation has

historically been especially heavy for mothers of boys. My friend poet Fred Marchant was once a lieutenant in the Marine Corps, and then an honorably discharged conscientious objector to the Vietnam War. He records in his poem "Wartime" a moment in a boy's training in independence and qualities we associate with it such as fortitude and endurance:

> Here in Belmont, the paperboy rings our bell
>   saying he's got the flu,
>   and could we call his Dad to take
>   him home. It is wet,
>   January, but Dad does not thank me.
>   He is disappointed in Mikey . . .

These days the standard applies as much to girls as to boys. Our idea of the admirable girl includes the same expectations of strength, self-sufficiency and emotional independence that have been the measure of a boy's excellence. Being the mother of girls and not boys doesn't protect someone from grappling with this very basic issue in a mother's life.

In my current thinking it is important to accept that we need to meet both kinds of needs as they are expressed by our children, fully and without reservation. I try to blur the distinction between dependence and independence by giving up the idea that dependence is only a means to becoming independent. They aren't opposite ends of a continuum, but states of being that can coexist quite harmoniously if we can alter our perspective.

I didn't arrive at this way of thinking in a flash, but bit by bit, one thought-provoking incident at a time. One experience in particular stands out in my mind as moving me toward this different viewpoint in the matter of rearing an independent child. It began one morning at seven o'clock. My closest friend and I had just finished a brief discussion of whether Rachel's interest in (and according to her teacher, talent for) gymnastics should be encouraged. She listened to my argument as to why not, and then said, "But she loves gymnastics. Anyone can see that."

I was still thinking several hours later about our conversation. Perhaps I hadn't described what I saw at the last gymnastics class clearly enough, expressed my alarm vigorously enough at watching Rachel's slender arms give way and the full force of her forty-seven pounds seeming to fall squarely on her neck and head. Seeing her fall, my body jerked back with such force that I slammed my head into the concrete wall behind me. We were both rubbing our heads when I saw her look to her teacher, who in a practiced, even tone, and with an utterly impassive face said, "You are all right aren't you, Rachel." I do not think my ears were playing tricks on me. It was not a question I heard, but a statement. I watched Rachel struggle to hide her tears, ignore her obvious pain and show her teacher what she wanted to see. Not a lovely, fluid cartwheel this time, but the confirmation that she is "all right" when she is not. This scared me.

I wanted to stand up and yell, "No, she is *not* all right. Can't you see that?" But I did not. I was silent, fearful of

being seen as a crazy, overreactive, interfering, overprotec-
tive mother. Instead I sat, my head throbbing, trying not
to think of Kerri Strug, the eighteen-year-old American
Olympic gymnast performing her final vault on an ankle
severely injured just a moment before, the coach's instruc-
tions to "shake it off" ringing in her ear, and wondering if
her pursuit of a gold medal had begun in a place like this,
a cavernous old warehouse festooned with championship
banners, the air layered with the odors of chalk dust and
sweat. But most of all, I was trying not to think of the
adolescent girls I have seen in my clinical practice who
have slowly grown deaf to the needs of their bodies, and to
the pain of wounds self-inflicted with razor, cigarettes,
laxatives and diuretics. They have told me their bodies do
not belong to them; that they are detached curious ob-
servers of sensations disconnected from hurt and alarm.
They learn this, they tell me, because their cries have been
met only with indifferent, unflinching eyes, met with
eyes that fail to see anything other than what they desire,
or met with falsely solicitous phrases that are really saying, "You are all right."

Over the many weeks of gymnastics classes I had become accustomed to Rachel's strong, clear voice asserting
itself predictably and frequently over those of the other
children, "Sue, look at me!" "I can do it, Sue! Look at me!"
As a baby she weaned herself at seven months. At one, she
sweetly but firmly demanded a cursory kiss and my hasty
exit from her room before nap and bedtime. She would
laugh gleefully and with pride at the story of her elfin

twenty-one-month-old voice repeating, "Shut-Door-Mom" well before I was finished singing her nighttime lullaby. She is a child for whom independence is exhilarating, and for whom there has always been particular pleasure in moving fast, of making her body hurtle swiftly through space. As a toddler, she jumped from any precipice she could find, and when she was two would point to birds and weep with frustration, telling us she wanted to be a bird too because she wanted to fly. Then one Saturday in October when the sky was sparkling blue and the buildings and trees lay flat against the horizon, Rachel leapt up at the moment her swing reached its apogee, she later told us, to grab the spire of a distant church. Launched into the air like a rocket, she plummeted face first onto the hard wooden deck below. My sister carried her into me, dripping from my morning shower. I saw her mouth, a bloody raw mess, one front tooth gone, the other dangling. "Mommy, it hurts," she said. It became a mantra. Rushed to a dentist we did not know, she was strapped into a restraint so he could suture her gum. We had to leave the room. It was better for her, they said. Her screams were piercing at first, but then they stopped.

———

Rachel's story of how she lost her front teeth changes from telling to telling, but the theme does not. If you ask, she will tell you that she was in her swing and her sister pushed her too hard, or that her father, who was not at home at the time, let his attention wander, and she fell. It is never an accident. And there is always a guardian entrusted with her safety who failed her, exposed her to danger and the humiliation of a gapped tooth smile she was not supposed to have yet, of the sensation of something missing, of a parent's lapsed watchfulness.

Since then, if she is hurt, she does not comfort easily. Her inconsolation is hard on all of us. Sometimes it has helped Rachel to be reminded that the pain of a new injury will stop, not go on and on as it must in her memory. I become upset when I realize I do not know what happened on her side of the door, how she felt, immobile and alone. But I do see that this break has brought forth a vulnerable part of Rachel, one that is hidden most of the time from public view, and one that might easily be hidden from mine, if I make that choice. I am left holding contrary images of my child, of this vulnerable little self and of a child who, if encouraged, would risk bodily injury to feel the thrill of having her stamina and fortitude admired by others. Which do I choose?

For many, the fact that she loves gymnastics should be enough. How could I possibly deny her this pleasure, this chance to feel like a star? I should tell myself to look upon gymnastics as Rachel's opportunity for graceful physical expression, the reinforcement of the importance of exercise, and pleasure in ever increasing mastery of her body. It is a vehicle to acquire self-discipline, to learn to remain undeterred in the face of adversity, and how to take her licks without complaint. I couldn't deny these as valuable lessons.

Nonetheless I felt unsettled, tangled up in thoughts and feelings unfurled by that infinitesimal exchange between my child and her teacher. I couldn't shake the feeling that there was more than a question of Rachel's development; something made it feel like a test, a test of whether I was a good mother, a good mother and a strong woman. One who does not interfere with her child's healthy self-assertion and supports, without fail and without question, a child's self-sufficiency and independent thought and action. A mother who can steel herself against the impulse to protect in order to let her child grow up, grow stronger, grow tough.

I found it hard not to see the exchange between Rachel and her gymnastics teacher, however small, as conforming to a pattern of human relationships that I help patients struggle to undo. I could well imagine her turning away from her perceptions in favor of another's. An act of self-denial to secure attention and acceptance and praise. The distinguished attachment theorist Inge Bretherton writes that relationships which support an easy give and take between parent and child depend on the parent "not selectively discouraging signals of distress." And many clinical theories of psychopathology suggest subtle pressures on a child to abandon perceptions and feelings to preserve relationships creates a sense of self which is "false" or "inauthentic." If I ignored what I saw, ignored what I knew about Rachel, I worried she would begin to disdain her vulnerabilities, regard them as shameful, and she would hide them from me, believing their expression weakens my esteem and love for her. The thought that I might not be a safe place any longer gave me great pause.

———

For all the glowing compliments about Rachel's strong, self-assured spirit, I knew then and now that little girls are never always strong, never always self-assured. I know this not abstractly or secondhand, but because I was a child that seemed to others to possess a natural maturity, self-assurance and self-sufficiency. A child who at five could be trusted to board the church bus with my younger sister on Sunday morning at nine so we might draw crayon pictures of Bible stories and hear Miss Evelyn tell me what a brave and responsible girl I was. A child impressed with the principle of *gaman* (endurance) who could sit stoically in the cold wind off Lake Merit, the seven younger children huddled under the picnic blanket for warmth.

It is difficult for me to imagine it could have been otherwise. I think of my aunt's stories of the physical endurance demanded by a farming life, her speed and stamina as a laborer unaltered by her fancy Eastern college education. I was well trained by the time I was six and on a train to Los Angeles, sick and feverish with the chicken pox. I did not call out to my mother, and passed the long ten hours by watching my sister and brothers toss a crumpled wad of paper back and forth between the seats. I can close my eyes today and see the erratic arcs and falls of that newspaper sphere, hear the giggles and shouts, my mother's gentle "ssh." I know how easy it is to become impervious to pain, and know the inward turning, the indifference to self, that one must cultivate. It becomes a retreat not merely from sensation, but a retreat from others.

————

Rachel took a break from gymnastics. We put her leotards and footless tights away for a while, knowing that there would be new challenges elsewhere, new opportunities, new and wonderful things to dazzle and excite her. There were those who questioned my judgment, those who worked the cost-benefit analysis to arrive at a different outcome, and saw me as a mother who betrayed the implicit promise not to interfere with my child's individuation, separation, autonomy, her self-reliance. But I decided that was okay. I figured I could take it.

LESSONS ON SUSPENDING OUR DESIRES

On repeated occasions, attention calls for a kind of radical self-renunciation . . . But such renunciation, necessary at moments, is not identical with attentive love. To court self-denial for its own sake perverts rather than expresses attentive love . . . The soul that can empty itself is a soul that already has a known, respected, albeit ever-developing self to return to when the moment of attention has passed.

Sara Ruddick, *Maternal Thinking*

THE DILEMMA OF EQUITY

According to my Webster's dictionary, the word equity comes from the Latin *aequus,* meaning equal or fair. When we say something is equitable, we are describing a situation in which all parties are treated equally. Playing fair, letting everyone have a turn, making sure no one gets a bigger or smaller piece, share and share alike. These are all rules we learn from earliest childhood about how we are supposed to treat one another. Most women today naturally assume that when she and her partner have a baby the responsibilities to care for that child will be shared equally and fairly.

Yet many young mothers know from their own experiences that this isn't usually how it works once a baby arrives. Research consistently shows that when men become fathers they become more firmly identified with the traditional role of breadwinner, and women find themselves, many quite unexpectedly, in the complementary traditional role of managing the household and looking after the baby. In spite of the expectation that a baby will bring a couple closer together, the birth of a child often introduces a greater separation instead. For women with traditional views about the roles of men and women, these differences in childcare and household responsibilities match their expectations of marriage and motherhood. However, for many others their experience is much more like that of this mother of two: "I have a very supportive husband, but I still run the household. I still have to make all the decisions. . . . Even if he does the shopping, I write the list. . . . I take responsibility for what we're going to have for dinner, to make sure the clothes are done. . . . And on top of that I go to work three days a week. And on the days off, I still have two children to look after. . . . My husband just doesn't even think of it. It's a different world to him."

Whether or not a mother works outside the home, and whether or not her partner endorses an equitable childcare arrangement, she still devotes more hours to childcare and household responsibilities than he does. In spite of all the changes in gender roles over the last twenty years, research consistently finds that married women with children devote anywhere from eleven to thirty hours per week more than men to their jobs, childcare and housekeeping.

In addition, there are regular differences in the kinds of household tasks men and women typically perform. Traditional male household responsibilities include chores such as household repairs, yard work and automobile maintenance. Research has shown that because these are done intermittently and are more flexibly scheduled, they are less stressful than traditional female household chores such as cooking meals, cleaning and picking up after children. Women's household duties are less discretionary. They are done daily and usually at very specific times of the day. These kinds of tasks have been described as "high-pressure, low-control" and are associated with greater levels of stress, anxiety and depression when compared to the "low-pressure, high-control" tasks of husbands. And as is true in every society in the world, mothers in America have the primary responsibility to care for the children in a family.

Developmental psychologist Michael Lamb and his colleagues summarized a large number of studies comparing men's and women's parenting activities. They found that mothers interact with their children three times as much as fathers, and are twice as likely to be the parent available to them even when they are not interacting with them. Mothers are ten times more likely than fathers to accommodate unexpected or seasonal changes in a family's routine. She is the parent who leaves work to take a child to the doctor, stays home with the children when no one else is available, arranges for nonparental childcare or takes the children to lessons, sports practice and social events.

Even when women anticipate managing more of the childcare tasks than their husbands, the extent of the inequity often surprises them and can become a source of conflict and tension. A friend points out the time related to the children, mostly unacknowledged and certainly unpaid, that mothers take responsibility for—the face time with schoolteachers, music teachers, soccer coaches, the trips to the library and office supply store for materials for school projects and, of course, the time on the telephone calling other mothers to arrange play dates, carpools and class activities.

Living this well-documented and common reality of motherhood also took me by surprise. My notion of the relationship between men and women was formed by a particular era of the feminist movement, and my ideas about shared parenting were strongly influenced by the feminist social critiques of Nancy Chodorow, Dorothy Dinnerstein and Adrienne Rich. As I thought about becoming a mother, I wanted my marriage to exemplify the feminist goal for families. According to the feminist family agenda of the '70s and '80s, that goal was for fathers and mothers to become interchangeable caregivers to their children, neither one more comfortable or skillful at the tasks of childcare than the other. This vision of family life was feminist because it was a piece of the larger struggle for equality between the sexes. The argument was that if women were to participate freely and fully in the world of labor outside the home, men needed to participate as full partners with women in the rearing of children, not merely as their complements, but as their equals.

Chodorow's book *The Reproduction of Mothering* was especially influential not only to me, but also to many other women grappling in the late seventies with the question of why the inequality in caring for children and the home existed. Her psychoanalytic perspective on the parent-child relationship fit neatly with the theoretical models I was familiar with from studying psychology. Her assertion was that familial inequality existed not by virtue of separate roles, but because the roles created two, separate psychological contexts in which children learn how they are to be parents themselves.

In Chodorow's view, when social norms dictate that women nurture children and men do not, girls acquire the psychological and affective capacities necessary to the care of infants and children, but boys do not. Dividing up responsibilities exactly down the middle, into a world of mother's work and a separate world of father's work, does not create the kind of equity considered ideal, namely that children regard their mother and father psychologically as equivalent caregivers.

The feminist family arrangement made sense to me. It was equitable, it seemed fair. More than I realized I carried this model of coparenting along with its ideological urgency into my vision of my life as a mother. But once I became a mother and I tried to put this ideal into practice, it was pretty quickly apparent that something was wrong. The problem was my husband didn't seem to have the same ideal in mind. I often puzzled over how to reconcile my vision of domestic equality with my day-to-day life with a man who fit the pattern researchers consistently affirm, acting out his role of father in a more traditional fashion than either of us ever anticipated. I kept trying to come up with guidelines for equality that would be useful in the mundane, reoccurring aspects of life between women and men once they become mothers and fathers. But it was hard to come up with ones that felt satisfactory. Most of them seemed to be some variation of a scorecard, with one column marked His and one marked Hers. I could always tell I was operating in this amorphous terrain when I began to dwell on questions about my husband such as, "Why is it necessary for me to remind him to feed the baby? Where the diapers are? When bedtime is?"

For a long time I would not allow myself to regard this need for guidance as anything other than a consequence of personal failing, a need I should suppress because I feared it revealed a lack of good judgment and understanding about my partner before entering marriage and before having children. Any time I thought to express it, I would find one or another popular aphorism about the necessity of stoic and mute acceptance of one's personal choices staring me down, steely-eyed and unblinking:

You made your bed; now lie in it.
Just make the best of it.
No whining. (Especially, no whining.)

I don't think any more that I was plain dumb to have interpreted my husband's desire for a partner with goals and aspirations outside the home, or his holding political beliefs about equal rights, pay and economic opportunity for women, as evidence of our having a common vision of equity in the management of our family life. It seemed it would be a natural extension of his other convictions. That's not the way it turned out, and as the research shows, in this way we are no different than the average, enlightened, liberal, American couple.

I do recognize now that my struggle with this issue of our domestic and childcare inequality was probably made more difficult because I did not grow up in a traditional two-parent family. My parents were separated when I was seven and at that time my mother returned with her four children to Los Angeles to live near her own family. Not in words but in practice, she conveyed that the world need not be separated into two, a world of men and a world of women, with one, sometimes the other, depending on the circumstance, being valued more highly than the other. She taught my sister, brothers, and me that all responsibilities were shared responsibilities, there was no such thing as jobs for a boy and jobs for a girl. My brothers did laundry, cooking and ironing, not as preparation for the time when they would be "on their own," but because they were expected to contribute equally to the smooth running of the household. My sister and I worked in the garden and took our turn taking out the trash, again not in preparation for the possibility that we might not have a man to depend on to accomplish these chores, but because everyone needed to learn to do everything. She created a home where consideration of others' feelings, and setting aside one's individual desires for the sake of the whole was expected of everyone, not just the girls.

The microcosm of my immediate family was mirrored in the extended family of my mother's brothers and sisters. I saw that my uncles cooked meals, cared for children, purchased groceries and gifts. Expressions of attentiveness and concern were not deemed the exclusive province of sisters and wives. My childhood experience of family life left me quite ill prepared for the traditional domestic arrangement that I found myself living in after Emily was born. In fact, a good deal of the time I felt like Gregor Samsa of Kafka's *The Metamorphosis*. One day I was an independent woman in a marriage where mutual respect and support of one another was freely given. Then I had a baby and I spent a lot of time in a topsy-turvy domestic reality, bouncing around in the confines of my sleep-deprived head, figuring out what the new rules were and trying to decide if they felt fair or not.

Looking back on those early years I did not really appreciate what a big life transition my husband and I were making by becoming parents. In trying to cope with the practical concrete details of life with a baby and our sense of new responsibilities, we gravitated to the models that we knew best, the ones from our respective childhoods. But since you probably could not have devised two more dissimilar sets of expectations, mine of a collectivist family unit where everyone knew how to and did everything, and his of the traditional division of a father's labor outside the home and the mother's as within, we misunderstood one another a lot. We didn't recognize it at the time, but like many first-time parents, we were struggling to come up with a new understanding of our partnership and responsibilities to one another, one that did not depend on principles such as "a tit for tat," or other accountant-type approaches. We needed to forge a new understanding of fairness, one that did not depend on splitting things right down the middle, or principles such as share and share alike.

My training as a psychologist and as a therapist inclined me to look to intrapsychic and interpersonal explanations to help me sort through the confusing imbalance of my family life. This perspective was often not as useful as an understanding of some of the forces outside rather than within marriage that create and maintain the domestic inequalities in most young families. Social scientists of several disciplines have studied this issue for some time and generally agree that biological, economic and sociocultural factors all play a role in the disparity between the work of mothers and the work of fathers.

BIOLOGICAL FACTORS. Because of differences in reproductive biology, men and women are inclined toward different roles vis-à-vis a newborn child. A woman's capacity to bear children and breast-feed them encourages an early asymmetry in the investment of time and physical and emotional resources each parent makes. Pregnancy gives mothers a preview of what the baby will be like. As a mother develops a sense of his or her rhythms, activity level and sleep patterns, she is already learning about her child before he or she is born, an opportunity her partner does not have.

Breast-feeding becomes another avenue mothers but not fathers have available to learn about their infant. Every nursing mother has stories about her baby's idiosyncratic snorts and smacks, habits and preferences. Babies who doze in the middle of a nursing session. A baby who pools milk before swallowing; a baby who needs to be sucking to produce an uninterrupted stream. Nursing mothers and their babies also establish a close and interdependent relationship as a consequence of the repeated cycle of baby's needing mother's milk and mother needing baby to nurse. Although attenuated somewhat, this pattern still holds true for mothers who bottle-feed their infants. A mother's biology gives her a window on her baby's budding individuality and an opportunity for intimate social interaction that fathers can rarely approximate, and sets the stage for a mother's closer involvement with a child for the first couple years after birth.

Whether they bottle-feed or breast-feed their babies, mothers generally spend more time in close physical contact with children than fathers do. They hold babies and toddlers more than fathers do. They also look, smile and talk with them more. This encourages fathers and mothers to develop different skills in interpreting a child's expressions and communication, with mothers generally becoming more adept at reading a child's signals and emotional states than fathers are. In turn, a mother's greater familiarity with her child's communication makes it more likely that in these first eighteen to twenty-four months she will be the parent the child turns to in times of distress. This often creates a circular process in which the father withdraws from interaction with the child, especially when the mother is present, because he feels he is less competent and effective in responding to the child's needs or demands.

I've often observed this dynamic when a father is attempting to get a child to cooperate and the child is refusing. Usually less familiar with the child's style of tantrums than the mother, he gets frustrated and gives up, loses his temper or resolves the impasse by asserting his power. The same kind of situation arises when a father, baffled by what his eighteen-month-old is asking him to get, turns to his wife who acts as the interpreter between them. The result is that mothers of infants and toddlers are much more involved with them, spend much more time with them, and feel more responsible for managing their routine and responding to their needs than fathers typically do.

The distinguished developmental psychologist Eleanor Maccoby suggests these differences in maternal and paternal sensitivity to a child's emotional signals are not merely a function of the amount of time a parent spends with a child, but reflect differences in women's and men's preferred styles of social interaction. Maccoby very elegantly and persuasively argues that female play and peer groups cultivate in girls greater skill in engaging in sensitive and reciprocal interactions. It is with their peers that girls learn how to interact with others in a manner that preserves good feeling and promotes collaboration. Researchers interested in the style of conversation between three- and four-year-old girls find even at this early age girls pay a great deal of attention to preserving good feelings between one another. For example, they make a point to acknowledge or agree with a partner's suggestion. When they make a suggestion of their own, they typically "soften" it by phrasing the suggestion as a question to avoid sounding coercive or demanding. For example, "I'll be the doctor, OK?" They often refer to themselves jointly, "We'll do," "Let's" or "Why don't we."

When preschool boys play together their interactions are organized around themes of dominance and establishing one's place in the status hierarchy of the group. Boys' play is more physical, and boys are more likely to use coercive and power assertion strategies to define their location within the male social system. In comparison to the interaction style of young girls, when boys talk to each other they use direct imperatives or prohibitions. They are more likely to reject a playmate's idea without reference to what the other child is doing. Exchanges between boys tend to be more domineering in that one boy issues orders or prohibitions and the other either simply remains silent or tries to withdraw.

These differences in preschool boys' and girls' typical styles of interaction are strikingly similar to differences researchers observe in adulthood when fathers and mothers converse with their newly verbal children. When compared to mothers, fathers are less likely to reply directly to what a child has just said or done, and are less successful at creating a conversational focus of mutual interest. In a study by T. G. Power that compared mothers' and fathers' style of engaging their seven-, ten- and thirteen-month-old baby's interest in a new toy, mothers "were more likely to follow up on their infant's natural curiosity . . . while fathers . . . often disregarded the infant's cues of interest and attention and often directly interfered with ongoing infant behavior." Mothers were "more likely than fathers to take an infant's attentional state into account and coordinate their own actions to suit it." The interactions between mothers and children maintain the mutual give-and-take characteristics established from the newborn stage through the rest of childhood.

While mothers seem to possess greater interpersonal understanding and sensitivity toward infants and toddlers, fathers are usually more interested in and skillful at interacting physically with babies and toddlers. Father's games with babies are likely to involve such activities as moving their limbs in ways that stimulate and excite the child. Fathers bounce and lift babies more than mothers. With preschool children, fathers are more likely than mothers to engage in rough and tumble play with both boys and girls. "Father play" consistently involves more chasing, rolling, tickling, play boxing and play wrestling. When children make requests of their parents for this kind of interaction, fathers are more likely than mothers to respond positively to the child's request.

In keeping with this preference for high-energy, physical interaction, fathers become more active participants after a child is able to walk and talk, usually around the time the baby is eighteen months old. From this point forward, the kind of physical style of interaction that men bring to fathering is better suited to the needs and interest of verbal, more physically independent children. This shift is reflected in mothers' comments such as:

"He hated just sitting around the house, watching her. But once he could carry her in the backpack, when he could take a nice long walk with her, he didn't mind taking her out by himself. Before that he was too nervous, maybe even awkward around her. As soon as she'd start to cry, he'd hand her over to me, no matter where I was or what I was doing."

"He's never been much into babies, but he really enjoys it when they can do things with him. I didn't know it the first time, but he really gets involved when the kids start running and swimming and playing sports. I know I just have to get through the first couple years and he'll start to kick in with this one, too."

It seems that the differences in men and women's reproductive roles incline them toward different kinds of involvement and styles of interaction with babies. In other words, the asymmetry of human reproduction enhances the probability that the mother and not the father will be the parent more closely involved with and familiar with the needs of a child, at least until the baby becomes less physically dependent and more verbally expressive.

ECONOMIC FACTORS. There is no question that men's greater earning power helps maintain the division of mothers' and fathers' childcare and household responsibilities, and can create the perception that a woman's unpaid labor within the family is less essential to the family's status and well-being because it is not compensated in hard cash.

The U.S. Census reports that between 1951 and 1997, the percentage of married women in the labor force nearly tripled, from 23 percent to 62 percent. Median income figures show that in 1998 women earned seventy-three cents for every dollar earned by men, based on yearly earnings of $25,862 for women and $35,345 for men. Women come closest to attaining earnings parity with men during the time they are twenty-five to thirty-four years old, earning eighty-two cents for every dollar earned by men.

In an economic system where women are on average paid less than men, when a couple becomes parents they are often forced to conclude that the mother and not the father is the parent who should reduce the amount of time at their paid employment. After having babies, women frequently redesign their jobs to be more compatible with the demands of childcare, further limiting their income as well as their opportunity for career advancement. It is often the case that when a woman is on a career path with fewer demands and is earning less than her husband, she is the parent whose income the family can afford to do without. This sets in motion the circular process of handing over the responsibilities of home and children to the woman, making it increasingly less likely that she will earn a wage comparable to her husband's. Many young couples who enter parenthood expecting to share childcare responsibilities equally eventually give up their plan as they realize the economic costs of doing so are much too great.

In an interesting paradox, some research suggests that women who earn more money than their husbands, or whose career demands are more intensive, do not have fewer responsibilities at home or with their children. Often this is because these mothers want to maintain a close, hands-on involvement with their children and end up "doing it all." But this situation can also arise because it is difficult to divorce ourselves from our deep-seated assumptions and attitudes about the appropriate roles of mothers and fathers.

SOCIOCULTURAL FACTORS. The disparity in wages men and women earn both reflects and reinforces the cultural expectations that women are primarily responsible for the care of babies and children and that men are the primary economic providers for a family. Having children brings a couple into closer involvement with social institutions—neighborhoods, churches, the workplace, schools and recreational clubs—that reinforce these traditional role expectations. These institutions form a necessary and valuable network of support and community for young families, but at the same time are often the source of criticism when men or women deviate from the social expectations of the traditional maternal and the paternal roles. Women whose work is central to their sense of themselves are still criticized for leaving their children in less capable hands, for being hard-hearted, and for placing their needs over the needs of their children. Whereas men who work part-time or are primary caretakers for the children are criticized for not fulfilling their responsibilities as the family's wage earner. As great as the pressures are on women to fulfill their socially prescribed roles as mothers, the pressure on men to conform to the conventional standard of fatherhood can be even greater. I have a colleague who is the most involved father I have ever known. An extremely capable and successful physician, he never discussed the extent of his coparenting in the workplace, realistically mindful that his male colleagues, most of them fathers themselves, would see him as deviating much too radically from the proper male role.

I read with interest a recent study of mothers' and fathers' emotional experience of their paid employment outside the home and their unpaid work at home. Psychologist Reed Larson and his colleagues found that fathers are significantly more unhappy than mothers when at their paid jobs. The authors of the study attributed this finding to the rigidity of the cultural expectation for males to define themselves and their adequacy as a father according to how well they fulfill the role as breadwinner. Fathers perceived their work outside the home as completely obligatory because of this unbending cultural expectation for men to be good providers, and therefore as more onerous, unpleasant and stressful than women's experience of their paid employment outside the home.

To my mind, the enormous influence cultural expectations exert on the role relationship between wives and husbands is vividly illustrated by two studies of alternative family arrangement. Bernice Eudisen's research on three nontraditional family forms—communal living groups, unmarried couples, and unmarried women—found that when a child was added to any of these family groups there was a shift toward greater social conventionality, including movement toward the traditional division of family labor. Nancy Radin's work on egalitarian families showed that when men and women reverse the traditional roles, and mothers become the primary wage earners and men primarily responsible for childcare and housework, the psychological and economic costs remain exactly the same, only experienced in reverse. In the families Radin studied, fathers reported the greatest cost of their nontraditional family was the loss of career advancement; mothers reported the cost to them was the loss of close involvement with their children.

These studies are particularly telling about the social and economic pressures on a couple making their transition to parenthood to align themselves with the traditional division of responsibilities in a family. For even when a couple makes a commitment to nontraditional family roles or a more egalitarian division of family responsibilities they nevertheless experience the psychological strain and economic costs associated with deviating from the culture's normative expectations for women and for men. Findings such as these underscore the conclusion drawn by Larson and colleagues that, "Full comparability between mothers and fathers is not likely to be achieved simply by changes in role behavior. Only when behavioral changes are coupled with change in deep-seated societal expectations and attitudes regarding appropriate roles for women and men are we likely to achieve a situation in which individuals can freely negotiate their responsibilities, irrespective of gender."

———

Figuring out how best to accommodate or adapt to the social forces that limit domestic equality challenges practically every young couple. I remain committed to the aim of an egalitarian family, although I am less idealistic than I once was. I no longer wave brilliant analyses of the benefits of wholly shared child rearing under my husband's nose (higher verbal intelligence scores; higher achievement scores in math; increased closeness between father and child; less anxiety, fatigue and stress for mother). It finally occurred to me that this was like taking a peashooter and trying to dismantle the Berlin Wall. Not that he was necessarily more obdurate than most men or dismissed this information as insignificant, only that I came to accept that I had just a tiny window on what he and I were wrestling with. For years, I had mistakenly assumed that just because he was a man, he somehow had more control over the social forces that invisibly maintain the private inequities of family labor.

I do some days still suffer those black cloud moments when the fiery rhetoric of "liberation now" creeps into my consciousness and I feel the rumblings of my old indignation start to overtake me. They usually descend upon me as I smell some part of dinner burning on the stove because I have been fielding telephone calls from work, signing field trip permission slips, initialing homework, working out a change in the baby-sitter's schedule, all before trying to get out of the door on time for a meeting. But I know these moments pass. I tell myself when you are part of a social movement that is proceeding at the speed of a glacier, you have to adjust your expectations about how fast you are going to get to where you want to be. I'm quite sure now that it won't be in my lifetime, and that is okay.

Reading a very brave and honest book, *The Conversation Begins: Mothers and Daughters Talk about Living Feminism,* gave me a chance to reflect on the evolution of my feminist ideals, and offered a valuable perspective on the matter of domestic equity. More important, it reminded me of some extremely useful insights my clinical work with families has given me:

One, feelings of anger and frustration that we think we manage to keep from our children are *never* a secret.

Two, children do not benefit from sustained conflict between their parents. This is especially true for young children who have yet to develop the skills necessary to grasp and make sense of the complicated, emotionally opaque sources of disagreements between adults. Parents can unwittingly impose on a child the burden to resolve what parents cannot resolve between themselves, and this includes the tensions and conflicts about the division of household and childcare labor within a family.

And three, most ideologies, feminism being one, that animate a sense of who you are as a woman aren't always compatible with who you need to be once you become a parent. They don't fit well because no matter how virtuous the social cause and its goals, social-political visions oftentimes are fueled by the notion that there is an enemy to fight and overcome. In principle they seek to bring about a better social order, but in application can become as narrow and limited as the view they attempt to alter. The result is impasse and conflict where trust and mutual accommodation need to exist.

Alix Kates Shulman, one of the mothers who wrote about her feminism in *The Conversation Begins* speaks to this point: "No longer the submissive, compliant wife we had both expected me to be when we married and had children, I fought back, even though my ideal had been the gentle family I'd been raised in. My husband was a fierce fighter, and in fighting him I became fierce myself—something I now regret. . . . Back then I thought that my children could only benefit from those principles

I struggled so hard for. But what they experienced was conflict between their parents, not my principles . . ."

Her daughter Polly's experience of her parents was this: "Though they didn't get divorced until I was in my twenties, I can hardly remember a time when my parents didn't seem to hate each other. . . . At the time, my mother used the terms of feminism to explain their war, calling my father a 'sexist tyrant' and other politically charged names, which seemed to fit him fairly well. . . . My mother says that they tried not to fight when we were around, but I heard them whispering and saw them trying to kill each other with glances. . . . I knew it wasn't my fault my parents hated each other, but I was miserably depressed and hated myself. I spent a lot of time being sad privately. I thought I was sad because the girls in my class were mean, or because I was bored at school, or because I hadn't done my history paper. I never considered that I might be unhappy because my mother and father were fighting. That would have been a betrayal."

Christina Kline, daughter of Christina Baker has a similar story: "My mother, Cynthia and I began to define ourselves as feminists at the same time. Mom was thirty, I was five, Cynthia was four. Mom would tell Cynthia and me what she was reading and what she was thinking, and it all made perfect sense to us. Of course women should be paid the same as men for the same work. Of course the princess Atalanta should be free to marry whomever she chose. Of course Daddy should stop treating Mom like a second-class citizen.

"But this was where it became difficult. As my mother became more involved in the women's movement, the ferment between my father and her increased. He spoke quietly and caustically, and often with an amused eye toward his small audience; she screamed and cried and smashed butter dishes against the kitchen wall. It was more fun to laugh with Daddy than to cry with Mommy, so our allegiance was divided. If we simply accepted that he was a jolly, benign presence and she was overly sensitive, then we wouldn't have to face the frightening possibility that the entire structure of our family might have to be dismantled."

Like the mothers of these two women, I used to worry about what my daughters would learn if I didn't challenge the traditional division of labor between mothers and the fathers. I was conscious of them watching their parents, taking in the way things were divided up between us. I wondered what they made of it, and what kind of images of partnership they would take into their young womanhood and their motherhood. I would ponder this question in ways that became a preoccupation, a filmy barrier composed of mental tally marks through which I gazed out on my family.

Becoming parents requires us to revise some of the ideas we have been taught to cherish from childhood if harmony and fairness are to flourish in family life: the principle that everyone has personal rights, personal autonomy and is therefore entitled to assert his needs and is entitled to parity on demand. The principle that we must be watchful of our individual self-interest, making certain that when we divvy up the bag of jelly beans we must make the numbers come out exactly even in order to be fair and equal. These childhood rules of engagement don't work very well in a family, a social system that depends on cooperation, compromise, accommodation and trust in the other person's sense of fairness to work well.

I tend to think that the tensions that can erupt around the equity issue in young families aren't solely about how mothers and fathers achieve parity in their workloads, although it is justifiably about that on some occasions. Rather I think they are about whether the cooperation, compromise and accommodation that are essential to harmonious family life are expressed equally by husband and wife, and eventually, by the children, as well. In the history of the American family, deferring, doing without and placing the needs of another before one's own, cleaved along gender lines. Generations of girls were raised to believe their selflessness was the moral center not only of their families, but of the entire nation. This is the inequity that feminists protested against. Fortunately, we don't have to raise our sons and daughters in that tradition any longer. We have a choice. That is something that feminism has accomplished for us all.

These days I remind myself that mutual respect and trust in the other parent for their contribution to the growth and happiness of a child is the goal parents must strive toward, and not an equitable distribution of labor. When I think this way the cloud that can descend from time to time doesn't seem quite as impenetrable. I know it will eventually thin. When it does, I can see more clearly that my responsibility as a parent is to look for places to invest care and attention where it will make a difference to us all, in ways that would move all of us forward with as much harmony as we can muster, even if we happen to be singing in different keys.

THE WISH FOR FREEDOM

Once upon a time I thought that a day would come and I would be a free woman again. When my girls were babies and the baby equipment seemed to be popping up around me as bright, cheerful and fast as bulbs in the spring, I imagined liberation would come when they were sleeping mostly through the night and eating solid foods. If I had been paying attention I could have guessed this wasn't going to happen. After all, there wasn't a Mother's Liberation Day sticker on the baby calendar I kept by my bedside. Baby's first visit to the doctor, baby's first smile, baby's first laugh, baby's first tooth. Not a single one that began "Mother's first . . ."

What I discovered instead of freedom was that my children needed me in ever more complex ways. They needed to be potty trained, and then taught how to dress themselves, a year later how to ride a tricycle, then a bicycle, and how to write thank you notes. The years slipped by. No matter how diligent I was, I couldn't escape the trail of reminders of who they had been but were no longer, the cast-off shoe, the outgrown clothes, the clutter of things hardly used. And it started to dawn on me that I wouldn't be a free woman ever again.

At first the thought that I wouldn't be free in the way I had been before I was a mother made me weak in the knees. It was overwhelming. I desperately wanted to know that some day I would have my premotherhood self back. I would longingly recall the time that I could have an uninterrupted telephone conversation, make a pasta sauce with tons of onions and garlic, or dash out at nine P.M. to see a movie and talk about it until two A.M. over a couple of bottles of wine. I'm not exactly sure what happened to those feelings of panic over losing a part of me that I took for granted and didn't know I would be giving up by having children. But those feelings that I was teetering on the verge of an existential faint have faded with time. Like the person who goes from living at sea level to trekking up Mount Kilimanjaro, I've acclimated to the thinner air.

It is true that I am well past the earliest phases of being a mother, the days of feeling my body didn't belong to me, the physically demanding days of power walking up four flights of stairs to our apartment with a baby flailing in one arm and the stroller slung over my back by another.

The days that required exquisite orchestration of competing wishes and needs. Yet I have no difficulty recalling that long stretch of mornings soon after Emily learned to stand that I showered with the bathroom door flung wide open because she would cry hysterically when I wasn't within sight. Every morning I'd wedge her Portacrib into the bathroom as far as it would go. She would stand in it, tears streaming down her cheeks, her arms outstretched pleading to be picked up. Her little legs pumped frantically up and down as if building up steam to launch herself out of confinement and into my arms. I remember sweating even as I was showering, poking my head around the shower curtain crooning, "Just one more minute, sweet pea," or hoping she would be distracted by a game of peekaboo. More than once after such a morning I arrived at work, sat down to have my first meeting with a student or a patient to find I had forgotten to take the Elmo and Big Bird Band-Aids off my knees and shins. Motherhood had turned me into a spastic shaver.

Emily and Rachel are now less dependent on me to do things for them and that has felt good. I can go for long walks and drives with them, go to the beach for most of the day and sit in restaurants, leisurely conversing and laughing rather than patiently building towers of McDonald's french fries and catsup with the younger child while the older one races around with a friend down the slides and into that pit of M&M-colored plastic balls. But I don't think that is the whole story. My feeling freer is not just about them getting older, although that helped. I say it isn't the whole story because while Emily and Rachel have been growing and changing in the most extraordinary, breathtaking, mind-boggling and wonderful ways, I have been, in the shadows of the riotous glory of their growing into themselves, changing too. Not outwardly but inwardly, in ways less obvious than theirs and in ways that often elude description. What I feel is that because of them I live in the world differently. Because of them I have become a different kind of person.

It isn't an entirely new me of course. A friend in graduate school whose family roots began in Scotland gave me a cookie stamp for Christmas one year. It was a small green ceramic square with the imprint of a six-pointed snowflake. He attached a note explaining that it was a tool for making Scottish shortbread (he included a recipe), and that it suited me because it was "pretty and efficient." If there is one certainty about hanging around with a bunch of smart, insightful people it is that you will be seen for who you are. He was right. I loved and still do love to feel myself efficiently working my way through my duties, uninterrupted and undistracted by requirements or needs other than those of the work itself. I find that state of being alone with my thoughts, of being unperturbed by others, deeply satisfying.

I am very sure that if I hadn't grown into womanhood at a time when there was greater assurance that a girl could claim an identity outside that of her family and then of her husband, at a time women did not need to curtail or suppress ambition or talent, I might not have been allowed to nurture such feelings. They might not have become "natural" to how I experienced myself as a woman and as a person. And without the counterculture stance that my grandparents took in believing daughters were as entitled and worthy of intellectual training as sons, my aspirations would surely have been muted, my Japanese cultural roots inclining me toward satisfactions in other ways of being in the world. But I was very fortunate. I grew accustomed to feeling pleasure in my freedom. Talking with first-time mothers, I sense that even more than I, they have been reared with the assumption that freedom of movement and choice and the sense of themselves as autonomous and self-directing are not privileges reserved for boys and men. It seems to me the notion that personal fulfillment involves being free and inviolable is a premise about their lives as natural to them as the rhythm of breathing. Being happy means being free, and whether we are prepared for it or not, having a baby limits that freedom.

Many women have strong intimations about the loss of freedom that a baby will bring even before they become pregnant. They hesitate about having a child because they sense that they will have to live a different way. One young mother expressed this awareness this way: "Just as my body had stretched and asked to bear this child, so my whole life—my relationships, my ambitions, and my self-image would have to re-work itself around the baby's presence."

A friend of mine named Brenda struggled for many years with the decision to have a baby. There was no deep dark secret behind her ambivalent feelings. Her mother had Brenda and her two brothers during the 1950s. It was an era when women of a particular social station were supposed to stay home with the children, finding their greatest fulfillment in creating a harmonious and efficient household. But Brenda knew that her mother's greatest fulfillment was not in her home, husband and children. It was in her work. "It was so obvious," Brenda would say, "her work made her the happiest. She just thrived on it."

Brenda never felt her mother did not love her. Their relationship never felt as black and white as that. A bright and perceptive child, what Brenda understood was that work gave her mother satisfactions that being a mother did not. All during her childhood she took for granted that like her mother she too would have work she loved, and that turned out to be true. But when she and her partner pondered the decision about whether she would have a baby, Brenda found it hard to imagine how she would preserve her happiness once she became a mother. Brenda knew intuitively what research on the transition to motherhood has shown. Almost all women perceive a "loss of individuality" when they become mothers, but women who have established themselves as psychologically and economically independent adults experience the most disruption to their sense of individuality. Sociologist Alice Rossi points out that for well-educated women who tend to defer the age of bearing their first child there may be a ten-year period of economic and psychological independence before becoming mothers.

Not every woman can envision the change in her sense of self that comes with motherhood. Some are firmly convinced that their children will be seamlessly incorporated into life as it has always been lived. Have Snugli, Will Travel. One first-time mother recalls she and her husband frequently repeated to others and to each other, "We're not going to change just because we had a kid." I remember my friend and colleague Tim proudly announcing the birth of his first child, a beautiful baby girl, and just as proudly telling me he and his wife Jen were confident they would continue their lifestyle, unruffled and undisturbed. They had resolved not to buy any products made just for babies, "No baby soap. No baby shampoo, no stuff just for the baby," he declared.

Needless to say that resolution didn't last long. Tim is now the father of three children, and he chuckles thinking back on his earnest, younger self. You can't escape the initiation as a parent. Sooner or later your children's needs assert themselves unambiguously. And you begin to have a sense that a child isn't like a houseguest whose preference for oatmeal rather than cornflakes you cheerfully accommodate because you tell yourself it is just a temporary adjustment. My friend Valerie tells the story of rushing to get her husband, the baby and herself ready to go to a very important party at the home of a prospective business client. The whole family dressed up for this very elegant cocktail party, and they looked stunning.

When they arrived at the house Valerie checked everyone one last time, her lipstick, her husband's tie, and the baby's diaper. Feeling certain they would make a terrific impression, she rang the bell. But when the door was opened it was with such a flourish that it startled the baby and she started to scream. And then Valerie's milk let down, soaking through to the front of her silk dress. She looked at that stain and it hit her that she had moved across a divide. "Before Children" (BC) and "After Children" (AC). It is a shift truly as monumental as any geologic upheaval in the earth's 4.6 billion years.

I suspect the "before children-after children" stories we are most familiar with are the ones of women who do not make it to the other side or those who can only get there by submerging themselves completely in their children. In our cultural history, mothers whose sense of self is merged with their children's are criticized less than women who go to great lengths to preserve the feeling that they are unchanged, untouched by the messy, sticky tedium of being with their children. These are the "really bad" mothers, the ones described in the early clinical literature as "narcissistically self-absorbed." They are the mothers we learn from the culture that we mustn't become: women without a drop of "maternal instinct," women who find their beauty more important than their children, "selfish," "immature" women who can't be bothered with their babies, and their modern day equivalent, the woman whose career is more important than her children.

I think about this mother whenever I read the *Eloise* books by Kay Thompson to Rachel. Rachel loves, loves, loves Eloise and interestingly has never once asked about

Eloise's absent mother. I think she is too absorbed by the fantasy that she is Eloise, racing against the elevator in the Plaza Hotel up to the fifteenth floor and back down, roller-skating down the thickly carpeted hallways, and reducing her tutor to tears. I, on the other hand, am intrigued by this nameless and faceless creature. Reading out loud on autopilot, I try to put myself into the place of that phantom mom. What a romantic life. Humphrey Bogart and Ingrid Bergman in *Casablanca* flicker on the movie screen of my imagination. And she is only thirty to boot. I am envious. We are reading about Eloise's dog Weenie and Skipperdee, the only turtle allowed as a pet at the Plaza, and I let my mind wander off to stories of other mothers who seem unable to bear the rumpled, messiness of living with children. Author Anne Roiphe writes this about her mother:

"I started writing my first novel with the picture of a child waiting outside a closed door. The child was me. I would lie on the carpet outside her room, my face pressed to the crack under the door. . . . I didn't play. I didn't move. I waited, my back pressed to the wall so nothing could grab me. She was there, I couldn't reach her. . . . When I was sick for long periods throughout the year with the earaches that would take me in those pre-antibiotic days, my mother would not come into my room. . . . I would wait for a glimpse of my mother, a flash of gold bracelet, a black hat with a net veil, pausing at the door. She would send me books. She was afraid of illness and would enter the room only when the fever was gone."

Roiphe's poignant recollection reminds me of Anna, a young mother I worked with in therapy. I imagine Anna's children will have memories like Roiphe's, memories of a beautiful, unhappy, emotionally remote mother whose true life did not include them. Anna came to therapy because she was depressed and anxious and because she thought she was a bad mother. She hated being a housewife and had fantasies of living a life of glamour and affluence, without the drudgery of housework, dirty diapers, cleaning up after her children, waking up in the middle of the night because of a bad dream, fever or worse. Guilt-ridden by the "lack of feeling" she had for her children she alternated between swooping in and kissing them and telling them she loved them and retreating from them as abruptly and unpredictably. She spent beyond her husband's modest salary trying to create the impression that she was a wealthy and pampered woman. She and her husband fought constantly about this.

Anna had described herself to me as a "mousey nothing" as a girl and teenager. To her very great surprise, in her early twenties she suddenly became a strikingly beautiful woman. Her parents and grandparents had discouraged her from going to college. So at the time this physical transformation took place she was working as a receptionist and living with her mother and father. She began dating for the first time in her life, and was both elated and terrified by the attention she was receiving from men. Life was easy and fun. She felt happy for the first time in her life.

Anna's parents, immigrants from Russia, were very troubled by her new and flashy lifestyle, one they perceived as alarmingly free of obligations and responsibility. They began to pressure her to get serious about one of the several men she was dating and to "settle down." Wanting to please her parents, but not having any idea of what she wanted or needed in a mate, she reluctantly followed her parents' advice and chose a man whose family belonged to the same church as theirs. She married a reliable, steady guy after a six-month courtship and became pregnant on their honeymoon.

In the course of therapy, Anna began to appreciate how angry and resentful she was about her marriage and about having children. She felt she was just becoming someone that people paid attention to, something she never dreamed would happen, when she was "forced" to give it all up. Although she had never consciously told herself so, Anna was living as though she had made a pact with herself not to let her husband or her children get in the way of being that glamorous, mysterious, desirable woman she felt she had been all too briefly before her marriage.

Slowly Anna began to see that she was resisting the inescapable. More important, she realized that if she was ever going to be able to move beyond her anger and grief, the chaotic feelings she had about being a mother and inconsistent way of relating to her children, she had to give up this fight for a lost self. We spent many weeks where she and I said very little and she just cried, letting go of that lost self. I think this letting go is what Jane Lazare

was describing in *The Mother Knot* about her own motherhood when she wrote, ". . . what filled me was the sort of
acceptance you feel one day after a loved one has died, and
the first passionate period of mourning over at last, you
say, Yes, he's dead. I must begin to live differently."

By letting herself grieve Anna was not as resentful
about her children and her husband and their needs, feeling less intensely that they were interfering with who she
imagined herself to be. But what took her most by surprise was that she no longer doubted that she loved her
children. She did. She realized she had loved them all
along, but only from a distance, without letting them get
too close to her. Intimidated by the message that she
needed to be a model of strength and confidence, accomplishment and independence for her daughters to grow up
healthy and strong, she didn't want them to know that
they had a "nothing" for a mother. Anna secretly feared
they would be disappointed by the person underneath the
makeup, jewelry, fancy clothes and perfect hair. It seemed
impossible that they could love her just the way she was.

As was true for Anna, freedom came only after I could
accept that my old life was gone forever. Before then I followed the common wisdom to "take care of myself." I
worked in regular breaks from the demands of mothering, arranging baby-sitting time, scheduling dinners and
lunches and breakfasts out to reconnect to an old self. I returned to my job and my professional identity. But until
I accepted my life before children was gone, these activi-

ties were merely momentary and tantalizing escapes, each little outing a wistful reminder of what I had given up.

Perhaps because as I looked at my life from the outside, it didn't seem as though I had changed at all—my professional life was unchanged and acquaintances seemed never to tire of pointing out that since I had made a career of taking care of children, being a mother was no different—it was a long time before I registered in what way I did feel different. Perhaps if we had a richly articulated theory about mothers' psychological development I would have felt less confused about what had happened to me. We know a great deal about pregnancy and the first year of babyhood and what mothers can expect. Morning sickness, the challenges of breast-feeding (sore and cracked nipples, engorgement), sleep deprivation, colic and teething. You can also find lots to read on every age and phase that our children go through after their first birthday. In contrast, we know so little about the inner, private world of a mother, or about what happens to her sense of herself. In the absence of such a theory, we tie a mother's thoughts and feelings so closely to the development of her child that we do not ask what a mother's experience of herself over time is. Without thinking, we assume that we must know everything there is to know about a mother's psychological growth just by knowing what is happening to her child. But, of course, that isn't true.

Without even being aware of it, I straddled the before children/after children divide for quite a while after Emily was born. Then one weekend afternoon when she was five months old we were home just the two of us, just hanging out. She was swinging happily in her crank-up Swing-O-Matic baby swing while I washed some dishes. I was wiping my hands after finishing the last pot and was walking toward her chatting about what we might do next when the color of her face went from creamy pink to chalky gray. She slumped forward and I felt my heart plummet like an elevator in free fall. I got to the swing, unfastened the safety clasp and laid her down. She was breathing, but was so limp and unresponsive, it felt like she was gone.

A neighbor drove us to the emergency room and the pediatrician there assured me she was fine. He thought she had just fainted. Maybe it had happened because she was in the swing, no one could say for sure what had caused it. But, he briskly told me, if it happened again, I was to elevate her feet above her head and she would spring right back to life, good as new. He was right about my baby. She seemed unaffected by her swoon and never fainted again. But as the mother of the patient, I can't say that I came away from that experience the same person I was before that baby faint.

In those few endless, terror-filled seconds that I thought Emily had died, I glimpsed a grief I had never known before. And in its wake a love I had not reckoned with either: tumultuous, ferocious, awful in the way that Miss Adams, my Latin teacher, taught her students about that word. Full of awe. That moment was the beginning of my giving up my sense of invulnerability, the feeling that I was master of my feelings, able to choose whom I would get close to, whom I would love. Before then, I had chosen my friends; I had chosen my husband. And only after a suitable period of getting to know one another did I give them my heart. Here was someone I had not chosen in the same way, yet my life was fastened to hers forever, and she would have my heart forever. Until that afternoon I do not think I had accepted that fact. I met up with an enormity of feeling for this tiny new person and knew at last that I could not be so moved and not be changed.

Over the years that love has made me a more rounded person, softened my angles and filled in some of the hollows and valleys. My friend Denise will say it has toughened her up, made her more focused and hard-headed in a way that pleases her. As a girl she spent a lot of time in the principal's office, but not because she misbehaved. She was a "regular" because she was the kind of kid who started out to school on time, then got distracted by the dragons and castles in the clouds and would lie down on a patch of grass, watching them as they drifted across the sky until her mother, having been called by the school, came to fetch her. Denise likes it that her children have made her less "out of step" with the rest of the world.

Being with my children has enlarged something within me, too. It has given me a chance to rethink the principle that I must remain the captain of my fate, in charge of my destiny at all costs. Every time Emily or Rachel reached out to be picked up, every cough, sniffle and runny nose, all their scraped knees, stuck zippers, bruised egos and hurt feelings have been a practice in making space for the "me" that is happy to give up being in charge, happy to daydream, stare out at the waves moving back and forth, in the here and now, receptive and responsive, loosening my grip on the expectation that I should be responsible, productive, forward thinking and forward moving. It is a "me" that now exists alongside the one that was raised to feel satisfaction and pleasure in autonomy and personal freedom of movement. I used to think I had acquired that extra pair of hands mothers dream about and eagerly vacation with parents and in-laws to have, even if only for a week. I felt lighter, yet I knew it wasn't because I had lost weight. I began to trust that I could let go of my private goals and aims, hold them in abeyance, and when that moment of being redirected by my children had passed, I would find myself. I could let my children impinge on me more freely because I no longer feared doing so meant I would lose myself.

I know from my students that this can seem a peculiar way to describe what happens between a mother and a child. Attachment, bonding and love they can deal with. Their eyebrows inch up slightly and then down and the identical worried wrinkle appears across their foreheads as they try to relate what I have said to something they have experienced. They glance down at my ordinary-looking black briefcase as though they have X-ray vision, wondering whether it contains incense, candles and audiotapes of one hand clapping smuggled in from Tibet. Someone, usually one of the men, breaks the silence by saying, "It sounds sort of like falling in love. That feeling that you are letting the boundary between you and the other person loosen." Then one of the women will say it reminds her of feminist theorists like Jean Baker Miller and Judith Jordan who speak about a sense of self that is not separate from, or merged with another, but a self that exists in relationship to others, a self-in-relation. We talk about psychoanalyst D. W. Winnicott's idea of "unintegration" as a state of being in which it is safe to be "nobody." This is a state of relatedness in between separateness and merger, a state of remaining connected to another while we let them find their own way, a way to be part of a whole, without the subjective experience of losing ourselves. I doubt that these ideas capture the experience of every mother. But I bring them up because it is good for mothers to have some alternative conception of selfhood, some notions of our maternal selves other than those of the self-contained, disconnected self, the narcissistically absorbed self and the self that exists only when "submerged" in the other. As I think back on those wise mothers it strikes me that they were describing the agility of moving in and out of this state of being "in-between." That growing into motherhood has meant learning to suspend their desire to think, feel and act purely on their own behalf, the desire to be unencumbered by another's needs and wishes.

It has seemed to me that it is harder to make this discovery about the state of being "nobody," a state of being in-between, if we try to be mothers in isolation from other mothers. Sometimes we keep ourselves more isolated than we need to because we are trying hard to live up to the standard and image of our premotherhood independence, a standard that says you have to do it all by yourself. Being connected with other mothers is an important way to affirm the complexity of mothering. These relationships give us a chance to share our knowledge, feelings and experiences that haven't quite made it into the culture's standard lessons on motherhood. If they are honest and open, they hold and support us while we learn to hold our babies. They give us the time among friends to recompose ourselves after the initial loss of self that is part of becoming a mother.

Being a mother has cultivated a greater ease in moving between the close attentiveness of being with my children, the experience of letting myself be a "nobody," and the experience of myself as forward moving, self-determining and free of others' needs and demands. When our first baby-sitter, Shana, was a little girl she and her brothers and mother, Helen, lived in the apartment next door to her mother's best friend, Susan, and her two children. The two families came to be like one, the children spending as much time in the care of their "other" mother as their own. Helen and Susan eventually cut a hole in the wall between the two apartments, a wonderfully literal dissolving of the formal boundary between the two families.

Life with my children has worn an opening between different parts of me. I have learned to go back and forth between those different selves without being too bruised, scraped or out of breath. Some days it is harder to make that inner passage than others, but doing so has given me the pure pleasure of knowing my children truly and well. It is a mother's reward for listening, looking and suspending desire. Learning to love my daughters attentively has been as much a frontier for exploration and discovery as those marked out in the world of my work. I am contented feeling my children are close to me, and that they find me someone they can trust. These days that counts for as much as anything I can think of.

As a new mother I wasn't certain that it was possible to strike a balance between a child's needs and a mother's freedom. I imagined the ideal as a constant equilibrium like the scales of justice in timeless, unchanging equipoise. When I finally gave up that unrealistic vision, one that curiously places children and mothers in opposition to one another, I wasn't embroiled in a private struggle about my freedom any longer. Instead I started to feel being a mother was like bobbing along in the middle of the vast and changing ocean: sometimes warm, sometimes cold, sometimes calm and sometimes not. Having been out here a while now, I accept that I'll never ride out the waves looking like Esther Williams—composed, effortlessly buoyant and elegant—but panting slightly and with stick-up hair. I am happy knowing that when those big waves roll in and wash over me, I'll come to the surface again. And when I do, I'll find a hand outstretched, warm and familiar, waiting for me.

EPILOGUE

Hearing Our Own Stories

Here is my story of how, no matter how we think it might turn out, the themes of our motherhood seem to hearken back to our mothers and theirs. For me, the variations move back and forth as in a fugue between words and silence, between these two languages of love.

————

Emily danced in a ballet recital for the first time in over three years yesterday. The program was to honor the mother of the ballet school's founder and director who had died quite suddenly and sadly six months before. The students rarely stage productions because the school's director believes their focus should be on the process, not the product, of dancing. The recital was therefore a very special event, and it was an honor for Emily to be asked to dance in it. Anna, her first dance teacher, had the seat behind me, and was quite pleased and excited when she noticed Emily name on the program. When the last notes of Beethoven's *Moonlight Sonata* were fading, and the dancers assumed their final positions, Anna leaned forward and whispered, "Oh, my god, she is so beautiful! I still think of her as a little girl."

I thought, "No, she is not a little girl any longer," and then of the poem I had read a few days earlier,

> *My daughter at eleven*
> *(almost twelve) is like a garden*
> *Oh darling! Born in that sweet birthday suit*
> *and having owned it and known it for so long*
> *now you must watch high noon enter*
> *as last month in Amalfi I saw lemons*
> *as large as your desk-side globe,*
> *that miniature map of the world,*
> *and I could mention too*
> *The market stalls of mushrooms and garlic buds*
> *All engorged. Or even the orchard next door*
> *Where apples are beginning to swell.*
> *And once, in our first backyard, I planted*
> *an acre of yellow beans we couldn't eat.*
> *but what I wanted to say, darling,*
> *is that women are born twice.*
>
> —Anne Sexton,
> "Little Girl, My Stringbean, My Lovely Woman"

Later that evening I was sitting where I am sitting now, preparing a flyer about the annual picnic at Rachel's elementary school. Emily, still in her leotard, was doing homework at the dining room table behind a vase of very tall purple flowers. Puzzling over the wording for the directions to the picnic, I heard her call me. I looked up. Her chignoned head was tilted just enough so I could see her face. "Why were you crying at the end of the piece?" she asked. I drew in a long breath and tried to collect myself by letting it out slowly. I had no idea she had seen me, there in the third row, safely ensconced (I thought) behind the director's family members, behind the very large family of the school's star student, Janine. It had only been a discreet tear or two, but she saw me.

I told her I had been crying because I felt such pleasure in seeing her dance, because she is so beautiful, so self-composed and graceful. She smiled back with delight. Then I screwed up my courage and told her I was crying also because I missed my grandfather who had loved Beethoven's music passionately, the Ninth Symphony his regular noontime accompaniment to lunch. It was always turned up full blast because he was growing deaf. As I was retreating into this memory, feeling proud of myself for being direct, clear about my feelings, she said, "Oh, I thought maybe you were missing your mom."

Then it was my turn to say, "Oh." "Oh" because it was so clear she was no longer a little girl. She was thirteen; when she said this, she seemed twenty-five. She knows me, too, now. "My mother is . . . ," she is probably saying to her friends over lunch, painting a word picture of her mother. It will be more like this from now on. So I have begun to wonder what new feeling her knowing gaze will bring me; and if I will bear honestly all that she sees.

Emily was right. I miss my mother. When she was diagnosed with ovarian cancer at the age of fifty-five, she commented how ironic that she had been until then so healthy, never a sick day from work; as a young girl, perfect attendance in Sunday school. No one was prepared for her to be sick. But I've learned no one is ever prepared, really, to lose someone you love.

The last time I saw my mother she was in the hospital. She had had a great deal of chemotherapy and repeated abdominal surgeries during her three-year treatment. Neither of us spoke about the fact that she would not be returning home. I sat in a padded hospital seat at her bedside, crocheting a receiving blanket for my sister-in-law. She leaned forward, I knew to look more closely at what I was doing, and opened her eyes wide, hopeful, questioning. I shook my head "no," and slowly she eased herself back, her slight sigh of disappointment mingling with the sigh of air from her pillows.

Her absence, now familiar, now accepted, will accompany me all the days of my life. This is not mourning unresolved, but an objective recognition, accepting myself as "me, with a dead mother I needed still." The familiar wish that she would have had the chance to watch her grandchildren grow up. But also the wish (is it selfish?)

that she could have looked upon me as a mother, too. I've missed having her know me in this way. I've missed being in her quiet presence, her capacity not to struggle, to be content and to find peace in the routine that was her life as a working mother with four children.

Talking figured so very little in my relationship with my mother. She did not do the things mothers are supposed to do to cultivate a sense of close understanding and intimacy. We did not share and confide in one another. She did not reveal herself in anecdote and reminiscences. Looking back upon her silences has felt like trying to catch sunlight reflected upon the placidly moving sea. Perhaps if she had lived through the first years of my motherhood with me, the situations would have led naturally to her telling me more about herself. But I know if she had, it would probably have been in fragments, spare, compact sentences, the kind of sentences I like to write that hint of something more hovering over the words on the page. I suspect I am unconsciously imagining a reader who is like my mother, one who never requires me to explain myself, because somehow she always knew.

As a therapist, I have been obliged to wonder if my childhood experience of sufficiency within her silence was merely an ephemeral figment of my imagination, in the world of psychotherapy, a defense against "true" feelings of loss, abandonment and loneliness. It never felt that way when I was with her. My children ask me to tell them about her. They always say, "your mom," a reminder that they have never claimed her as someone separate from me, never as someone that belongs to them. I have told them:

If you don't count the time I tried to persuade her that I could go on the Girl Scout camping trip with a case of the measles, we had only one true argument.

I never heard her yell at anyone.

She never complained, reprimanded, scolded or nagged.

She had a wonderful smile and a very hearty laugh for such a tiny woman.

My mother told me just once that she loved me. She needn't have. I knew that she did. When I look at my own children I see they need to hear about their mother's thoughts and feelings. Even if it wasn't necessary for me, it is for them. My mother's wordless expressiveness, her unspoken language of love would be insufficient and un-intelligible to my children. Some days I think that must be why I am writing this book, to put words to all that I have understood about love between mothers and their children. It is my way to put it down once, so I won't have to think any longer about how to say it. But I know this isn't how things this important work. The most valuable lessons in life aren't imparted or learned efficiently like the multiplication tables, once committed to memory, there, reliably, automatically and indelibly, but rather dis-covered and lost and discovered and lost again.

> *I have read each page of my mother's voyage*
> *I have read each page of her mother's voyage*
> *I have learned their words as they learned Dickens' . . .*
> —*Anne Sexton, "Crossing the Atlantic"*

The words on the page of my mother's voyage are few, of my grandmother's even fewer, but their silences are full and tender, graceful, beautiful and brave—not cold, vacant or threatening. It has taken time to give up the wish that my children would find sufficiency in my silence as I did in my mother's, that I would not have to be to them, other than my mother was to me. I gave it up because I want to make sure the story that my children write will be a story with love.

———

A mother's words and a mother's silence, these are the shores between which my voyage with my children, and their children, will meander. Emily tells me she loves me a lot; Rachel, hardly at all. I wonder if my mother ever thought about the kind of mother I would need to become, whether there was not some part of her story that foreshadowed mine. It is clearer to me that this story of love in two languages will be told and retold over and over in the generations to come, woven back and forth like the shuttle on a loom. The woof, the warp, together making a whole.

ACKNOWLEDGMENTS

I would like to thank my family and the many friends and colleagues who supported and encouraged me during the writing of this book.

Sara Ruddick's philosophical writings on mothers and children were an essential intellectual point of departure for the essays that comprise this book. Cynthia Garcia Coll, Janet Surrey and Kathy Weingarten made possible my participation in a Wellesley Centers for Women study group on mothers and resistance, an invaluable impetus toward clarifying my own perspective on mothering.

Jessica Henderson Daniel encouraged me with her gift of *Zenzele: A Letter for My Daughter* and its inscription, "May this inspire you to pursue your interests in writing about meaningful topics—ones that help people think, feel and understand." Her confidence in me has been an important touchstone in my growth as a psychologist.

Cutler Durkee and Barbara Watkins, gifted editors both, offered sage advice about making academic ideas accessible to a general readership.

Laura Benkov, Elizabeth Blumberg, Ellen Braaten, Leslie Gross, Cynthia Moore and Deborah Offner read the manuscript at various points in its development, each with care, insight and enthusiasm. Early on Stefi Rubin gave her gentle, yet completely thorough grasp of my aims. Fred Marchant provided exceedingly wise counsel at a critical juncture.

My lifelong friends Wanda Chin and Catalina Arboleda made me laugh and bolstered my spirits as only friends who know you really well can do. My sister, Judy Ohye, not only traveled across the country to free me to write, but also has lent her wonderful skills as a research librarian to locate esoteric articles and books; my brother Wesley Ohye has been an understanding, empathic listener. My daughters and my husband, Don, gave this project their generous and multiple blessings, and most of the time with good cheer, the time to think, read and write.

This book would not have been written without the creative vision and nurture of Joshua Horwitz. He has been an unflagging supporter and trusted adviser from its inception. I could not have asked for a more capable representative and advocate than my agent Gail Ross. Janet Goldstein, a superb editor, has been a patient and skillful guide. This book is a much better one for their involvement.

For many years, my patients and my students have freely shared their thoughts and feelings with me. In order to respect that trust and to protect their privacy, I have changed names and identifying details, as well as constructed composites.

My children asked that I not use their real names. Emily and Rachel are the pseudonyms they chose.

NOTES

Book Epigraph: Excerpt from "Water." Christopher Jane Corkery, *The Antioch Review,* Vol. 37, No. 4, Fall 1979.

Preface

Page

xiv   "standing on two shores . . ." Gloria Anzaldua, *Border-lands/La Frontera.* (San Francisco: Spinster/Aunt Lute, 1987): p. 78.

xv   "[find] herself in him." Sara Ruddick, *Maternal Think-ing: Toward a Politics of Peace.* (Boston: Beacon Press, 1989, 1995): p. 121.

xv   "wait to hear the answer . . ." Ibid., p. 121.

Listening Epigraph: ". . . even her silence was a kind of speech." Susan Griffin, *A Chorus of Stones: The Private Life of War.* (New York: Doubleday, 1992): p. 6.

Echoes

Page

12   "The patient does not . . ." Sigmund Freud, "Recom-mendations to Physicians Practicing Psychoanalysis," *Standard Edition of Complete Psychological Works of Sigmund Freud,* vol. 12. James Strachey, ed. (London: Hogarth Press and Institute of Psychoanalysis, 1958): pp. 111–112.

15   "The memory of . . ." Fred Pine, *Developmental Theory and Clinical Process.* (New Haven, CT: Yale University Press, 1985): p. 174.

18   "In every nursery . . ." Selma Fraiberg, E. Adelson and
            V. Shapiro, "Ghosts in the Nursery: A Psychoanalytic
            Approach to the Problem of Impaired Infant-Mother
            Relationships." *Journal of the American Academy of
            Child Psychiatry,* 14 (1975): pp. 387–421.

19   British psychoanalyst John Bowlby . . . John Bowlby,
            Attachment. (New York: Basic Books, 1969). This is the
            first of Bowlby's three-volume work on attachment.
            The second was titled *Separation,* and was published in
            1973. The third, *Loss,* appeared in 1980.

19, 21   Categories of adult attachment . . . Mary Main, N. Ka-
            plan and J. Cassidy, "Security in Infancy, Childhood
            and Adulthood: A Move to the Level of Representa-
            tion." In I. Bretherton and E. Waters, eds., *Growing
            Points of Attachment Theory and Research.* (Monographs
            of the Society for Research in Child Development, 50,
            serial no. 209, 1985): pp. 66–104.

23   "'How many hours do you have?'" Ibid, p. 96. *N.B.:*
            Main's research included fathers as well, but since the
            focus of this book is mothers, I refer only to the moth-
            ers in this summary of findings.

24   most notably that of Peter Fonagy. See, for instance, Pe-
            ter Fonagy, H. Steele, and M. Steele, "Maternal Repre-
            sentation of Attachment During Pregnancy Predicts
            Organization of Infant-Mother Attachment at One
            Year of Age," *Child Development,* 62 (1991): pp.
            891–905.

A Child Is Crying

Page

32   "to survive to . . ." Eleanor E. Maccoby, *The Two Sexes:
            Growing Up Apart, Coming Together.* (Cambridge, MA:
            Harvard University Press, 1998): p. 91.

36   During the 1960s . . . A more thorough presentation
            of these ideas can be found in A. Thomas, S. Chess and
            H. G. Birchy *Temperament and Behavior Disorders in Chil-
            dren* (New York: New York University Press, 1969).

37   Temperament refers to . . . William B. Carey, *Under-*

standing Your Child's Temperament. (New York: Simon and Schuster, 1997): pp. 12–13.

37 A baby's temperament is . . . Helen Neville and Diane Clark Johnson, *Temperament Tools: Working with Your Child's Inborn Traits.* (Seattle, WA: Parenting Press, 1998): pp. 53–55.

38 A milder child just . . . Ibid., p. 12.

39 Harvard developmental psychologist . . . Jerome Kagan and Nancy Snidman, "Temperamental Factors in Human Development," *American Psychologist,* 46 (1991): pp. 856–862. See also, J. Kagan, "Temperamental Contributions to Social Behavior," *American Psychologist,* 44 (1989): pp. 668–674.

40 "We suggest only . . ." J. Kagan and N. Snidman, p. 857.

40 For example, Ruth Feldman . . . See Ruth Feldman, C. W. Greenbaum, L. C. Mayes and S. H. Erlich, "Change in Mother-Infant Interactive Behavior: Relations to Change in the Mother, the Infants and the Social Context," *Infant Behavior and Development,* 20, 2 (1997): pp. 151–163, and also Ruth Feldman, C. W. Greenbaum and N. Yirmiya, "Mother-Infant Affect Synchrony as an Antecedent of the Emergence of Self-Control, *Developmental Psychology,* 35, 1 (1999): pp. 223–231.

Hearing the Unspoken

Page

59 "The rule for the doctor . . ." Sigmund Freud, "Recommendations to Physicians Practicing Psychoanalysis," *Standard Edition,* vol. 12, pp. 111–112.

65 Gusii mothers of eastern Kenya . . . Robert LeVine, S. Dixon, S. LeVine, A. Richman, P. H. Leiderman, C. Keefer and T. B. Brazelton, *Child Care and Culture: Lessons from Africa.* (Cambridge: Cambridge University Press, 1994).

65 these children hold their parents' attention . . . S. B. Heath, *Ways with Words: Language, Life and Work in*

Communities and Classrooms. (Cambridge: Cambridge University Press, 1983). Cited in B. Rogoff et al., p. 13.

66   In a widely cited study . . . B. Rogoff et al., *Guided Participation in Cultural Activity by Toddlers and Caregivers.* (Monograph of the Society for Research in Child Development, 58, 1993).

69   Adults in Guatemala . . . M. Nash, *Machine Age Maya.* (Chicago: University of Chicago Press, 1967). Cited in Rogoff et al., p. 156.

69   "Let me weave." J. Collier, Jr., "Survival at Rough Rock: A Historical Overview of Rough Rock Demonstration School," *Anthropology and Educational Quarterly,* 19 (1988): pp. 253–269. Cited in B. Rogoff et al., p. 156.

Looking Epigraph: "Land lies in water; . . ." Excerpt from "The Map." Elizabeth Bishop, *The Complete Poems, 1927–1979.* (New York: The Noonday Press, Farrar, Straus and Giroux, 1994): p. 3.

Goodness and Shame

Page

78   Social psychologists have studied . . . See, for example, Klaus R. Scherer and Harald G. Wallbott, "Evidence for Universality and Cultural Variation of Differential Emotion Response Patterning," *Journal of Personality and Social Psychology,* 66, 2 (1994): pp. 310–328; or Carroll E. Izard, "Innate and Universal Facial Expressions: Evidence from Developmental and Cross-Cultural Research," *Psychological Bulletin,* 115, 2 (1994): pp. 288–299.

83   "alternative excellences." Sara Ruddick, *Maternal Thinking: Toward a Politics of Peace,* p. 108. Here is this concept in its original context: "Her children's differences require the most demanding of a mother's many balancing acts: alongside her own strong convictions of virtues and excellence she is to place her children's human need to ask and answer for themselves questions

central to moral life. This means that she has to require of herself an appreciation of alternative excellences and virtues within her own family circle and within her own heart."

91   "never thought to . . ." Mark Epstein. *Thoughts Without a Thinker: Psychotherapy from a Buddhist Perspective.* (New York: Basic Books, 1995): p. 197.

94   Current psychological theory describes shame . . . See for example, June P. Tangney, "Assessing Individual Differences in Proneness to Shame and Guilt: Development of the Self-Conscious Affect and Attribution Inventory, *Journal of Personality and Social Psychology,* 59 (1990): pp. 102–111. Also Melvin R. Lansky, "Shame and the Score of Psychoanalytic Understanding," *American Behavioral Scientist,* 38 (1995): pp. 1076–1090.

Nature and Nurture

Page

107   "purely and unceasingly" Perry Miller, *The New England Mind: The Seventeenth Century.* (Boston: Beacon Press, 1939): p. 8.

108   "right action." Edmund S. Morgan, *The Puritan Family: Religion and Domestic Relations in Seventeenth-Century New England.* (New York: Harper & Row, 1966): p. 97.

108   "make an evil natured . . ." Ibid, p. 97.

109   "lewd and wild courses . . ." Cotton Mather, *Magnalia Christi Americana* (Hartford, 1985), II, p. 157. Cited in E. S. Morgan, p. 94.

109   "Eternal Vengeance . . ." Benjamin Wadsworth, "The Nature of Early Piety," in *A Course of Sermons on Early Piety,* p. 10. Cited in E. S. Morgan, p. 93.

112   One of the most important . . . This research is discussed in the following: W. Andrew Collins, Eleanor E. Maccoby, Laurence Steinberg, E. Mavis Heatherington and Marc H. Bornstein, "Contemporary Research on Parenting: The Case for Nature and Nurture," *American Psychologist,* 55 (2000): pp. 218–232.

113   example comes from Grazyna Kochanska's research . . . G. Kochanska, "Multiple Pathways to Conscience for Children with Different Temperaments: From Toddlerhood to Age 5," *Developmental Psychology,* 33 (1997): pp. 228–240.

118   Activity level in boys . . . Eleanor Maccoby, *The Two Sexes: Growing Up Apart, Coming Together.* (Cambridge, MA: The Belknap Press of Harvard University Press, 1998).

119   "behavior which hurts . . ." Eleanor E. Maccoby and Carol N. Jacklin, "Sex Differences in Aggression: A Rejoinder and Reprise," *Child Development,* 51 (1980): pp. 964–980.

120   "executive functions." For example, Jean R. Seguin, Robert O. Pihl, Philip W. Harden, Richard E. Tremblay and Bernard Boulerice, "Cognitive and Neuropsychological Characteristics of Physically Aggressive Boys," *Journal of Abnormal Psychology,* 104 (1995): pp. 614–624.

120   the concept of "relational aggression . . ." Nikki Crick, Nicole E. Werner, Juan F. Casas, Kathryn M. O'Brien, David A. Nelson, Jennifer K. Grotpeter and Kristian Markon, "Childhood Aggression and Gender: A New Look at an Old Problem." In D. Bernstein, ed., *Nebraska Symposium on Motivation,* 45 (1999): pp. 75–142.

124   "parenting style." See, for example, D. Baumrind, "Child Care Practices Anteceding Three Patterns of Preschool Behavior," *Genetic Psychology Monographs,* 75 (1967): pp. 43–99. D. Baumrind, "Current Patterns of Parental Authority," *Developmental Psychology,* 4 (1971): pp. 1–103; or E. E. Maccoby and J. A. Martin, "Socialization in the Context of the Family: Parent-Child Interaction. In P. H. Mussen, series Ed. and E. M. Hetherington, vol. ed., *Handbook of Child Psychology: Vol. 4. Socialization, Personality, and Social Development,* 4th ed. (New York: Wiley, 1983): pp. 1–101.

125   "[M]an does nothing by compulsion . . ." Perry Miller, p. 265.

126   "Give me a dozen healthy infants . . ." John Watson, *The Psychological Care of Infant and Child*. (New York: Norton, 1928). Cited in Judith Rich Harris, *The Nurture Assumption: Why Children Turn Out the Way They Do*. (New York: The Free Press, 1998): p. 6.

133   "And now outside . . ." Annie Dillard, *Holy the Firm*. (New York: Harper & Row, 1977): p. 50.

Independence and Dependence

Page

139   Alexis de Tocqueville. The first volume of de Tocqueville's two-part study *Democracy in America* was published in 1835, the second in 1840. This work is discussed in Robert N. Bellah, Richard Madsen, William M Sullivan, Ann Swidler and Steven M. Tipton, *Habits of the Heart: Individualism and Commitment in American Life*. (New York: Harper & Row, 1985): pp. 36–41.

139   "The society of which . . ." John Dewey, "Ethical Principles Underlying Education." In Reginald D. Archambault, ed., *John Dewey on Education: Selected Writings*. (New York: The Modern Library, 1964): p. 113.

140   "Carried to and fro . . ." John Demos, "The Changing Faces of Fatherhood: A New Exploration in Family History." In F. Kessel and A. Siegel, eds., *The Child and Other Cultural Inventions*. (New York: Praeger, 1983): p. 162.

140   "There was no question of . . ." E. S. Morgan, p. 97.

142   "When you are tempted . . ." John Watson, *The Psychological Care of Infant and Child*. In Nancy Pottishman Weiss, "Mothers, the Invention of Necessity: Dr. Benjamin Spock's Baby and Child Care." In N. Ray Hiner and Joseph M. Hawes, eds., *Growing Up in America: Children in Historical Perspective*. (Chicago: University of Illinois Press, 1985): pp. 283–303.

143   "One day when Michael . . ." Olga Silverstein and Beth Rashbaum, *The Courage to Raise Good Men*. (New York: Viking Penguin, 1994): pp. 2–3.

145   "Trust yourself." Benjamin Spock, *Dr. Spock's Baby and Child Care.* (New York: Pocket Books, 1945): p. 1.

145   "Nobody has to tell . . ." Louise Kaplan, *Oneness and Separateness: From Infant to Individual.* (New York: Simon & Schuster, 1978): pp. 120.

146   "The drive for . . ." T. B. Brazelton, *Toddlers and Parents: A Declaration of Independence,* revised edition. (New York: Delacorte Press/Seymour Lawrence, 1989): p. 223.

147   "If you expect . . ." Penelope Leach, *Your Baby and Child: From Birth to Age Five.* New York: Knopf, 1989): p. 285.

148   The research of feminist . . . Jean Baker Miller, *Toward a New Psychology of Women.* (Boston: Beacon Press, 1976). Writing on the ethic of care versus the ethic of responsibility: Carol Gilligan, "Woman's Place in Man's Life Cycle," *Harvard Educational Review,* 49 (1979): pp. 431–446, as well as Carol Gilligan, "In a Different Voice: Women's Conceptions of Self and Morality," *Harvard Educational Review,* 47 (1977): 481–517. On self-in-relation theory: Judith Jordan, Jean Baker Miller, Irene Stiver, Janet Surrey and Alexandra Kaplan, *Women's Growth in Connection.* (New York: Guilford Press, 1991).

151   *jibun* Hazel Rose Markus and Shinobu Kitayama, "Culture and the Self: Implications for Cognition, Emotion, and Motivation," *Psychological Bulletin,* 98 (1991): pp. 224–253.

151   "denial of the need of the other." This expression is from Jessica Benjamin, "Authority and the Family Revisited or, A World without Fathers?" *The New German Critique,* 13 (winter, 1978): pp. 35–57.

152   "Here in Belmont . . ." "Wartime," Fred Marchant, *Tipping Point.* (Washington, DC: The WORD WORKS, 1993): p. 50.

157   "not selectively discouraging . . ." Inge Bretherton, "New Perspectives on Attachment Relations: Security, Communication, and Internal Working Models." In

J. D. Osofsky, ed., *Handbook of Infant Development,* 2nd edition, (New York: John Wiley & Sons, 1987): pp. 1061–1100.

157   sense of self which is "false" or "inauthentic." See for example, D. W. Winnicottt, "Ego Distortion in Terms of True and False Self." In *The Maturational Processes and the Facilitating Environment.* (New York: International Universities Press, 1965). For a popular treatment of this issue, see for example, Alice Miller, *Prisoners of Childhood: The Drama of the Gifted Child and the Search for the True Self.* (New York: Basic Books, 1996).

Suspending Our Desires Epigraph: "On repeated occasions, . . ." Sara Ruddick, p. 122.

The Dilemma of Equity

Page

164   "I have a very supportive husband . . ." Susan Maushart, *The Mask of Motherhood: How Becoming a Mother Changes Everything and Why We Pretend It Doesn't.* (New York: The New Press, 1999): p. 177.

164   Whether or not a mother works outside the home. For example, Arlie Hochschild (with Anne Machung), *The Second Shift: Working Parents and the Revolution at Home.* (New York: Viking, 1989). Research conducted in the 1990s continued to find the same patterns, see for example, Marjorie Starrels, "Husbands' Involvement in Female Gender-Typed Household Chores," *Sex Roles: A Journal of Research,* 31 (1994): pp. 473–491, or Susan Mitchell, "Who Does the Shopping?" *American Demographics,* 18 (1996): pp. 56–57.

165   Developmental psychologist Michael Lamb . . . M. E. Lamb, J. H. Pleck, E. L. Charnov and J. A. Levine, "A Biosocial Perspective on Paternal Behavior and Involvement. In J. B. Lancaster, J. Altman, A. S. Rossi, and L. R. Sherrod, eds., *Parenting Across the Lifespan.* (New York: Aldine de Gruyter, 1987): pp. 111–42.

166   feminist social critiques . . . Nancy Chodorow, *The Reproduction of Mothering: Psychoanalysis and the Sociology of Gender.* (Berkeley: University of California Press, 1978); Dorothy Dinnerstein, *The Mermaid and the Minotaur: Sexuality and Human Malaise.* (New York: Harper Perennial, 1976); and Adrienne Rich, *Of Woman Born: Motherhood as Experience and Institution.* (New York: Norton, 1976).

173   The distinguished developmental psychologist Eleanor Maccoby. See, for example, E. E. Maccoby and C. N. Jacklin, "Gender Segregation in Childhood," *Advances in Child Development and Behavior,* 20 (1987): pp. 239–287.

175   In a study by T. G. Power . . . "Mother- and Father-Infant Play: A Developmental Analysis," *Child Development,* 56 (1985): pp. 1514–1524.

177   The U.S. Census . . . *Current Population Surveys.* (Washington, D.C.: U.S. Department of Commerce, Economics and Statistics Division. Bureau of the Census, 1998).

179   read with interest . . . R. W. Larson, M. H. Richards, M. Perry-Jenkins, "Divergent Worlds: The Daily Emotional Experience of Mothers and Fathers in the Domestic and Public Spheres," *American Psychologist,* 67 (1994): pp. 1034–1046.

180   Bernice Eudisen's research . . . Bernice Eudisen, M. Kornfein, I. L. Zimmerman and T. S. Weisner, "Comparative Socialization Practices in Traditional and Alternative Families." In M. E. Lamb, ed., *Nontraditional Families: Parenting and Child Development.* (Hillsdale, NJ: Erlbaum, 1982): pp. 315–346.

180   Nancy Radin's work . . . N. Radin, "Primary Caregiving and Role-Sharing Fathers." Ibid, pp. 173–204.

181   "Full comparability between mothers and fathers . . ." Reed Larson et al., p. 1044.

183   "No longer the submissive . . ." Alix Kates Shulman in Christina Looper Baker and Christina Baker Kline, eds., *The Conversation Begins: Mothers and Daughters*

Talk About Living Feminism. New York: Bantam (1996): p. 92.

184   "Though they didn't get divorced . . ." Polly Shulman, Ibid, pp. 97–98.

184   "My mother, Cynthia and I . . ." Christina Kline, Ibid, p. 11.

The Wish for Freedom

Page

193   "Just as my body had . . ." Nina Barrett cited in *The Mask of Motherhood,* p. 106.

194   "loss of individuality . . ." C. P. Cowan and P. A. Cowan, *When Partners Become Parents: The Big Life Change for Couples.* (New York: Basic Books, 1992).

194   Sociologist Alice Rossi . . . Alice Rossi, "Gender and Parenthood," *American Sociological Review,* 49 (1984): pp. 1–19.

195   "We're not going to change . . ." Christina Baker Kline, ed., *Child of Mine: Writers Talk About the First Year of Motherhood.* (New York: Hyperion, 1997): p. 204.

196   whenever I read . . . Kay Thompson, *Eloise.* (New York: Simon and Schuster, 1955).

197   "I started writing my first novel . . ." Anne Roiphe, *Fruitful: A Real Mother in the Modern World.* (Boston: Houghton Mifflin Company, 1996): pp. 5–6.

199   I think this letting go . . . Jane Lazare, *The Mother Knot.* (Boston: Beacon Press, 1985): p. 62.

205   reminds her of feminist theorists . . . Jean Baker Miller, *Toward a New Psychology of Women.* (Boston: Beacon Press, 1976). Judith Jordan, Jean Baker Miller, Irene Stiver, Janet Surrey, and Alexandra Kaplan, *Women's Growth in Connection.* New York: Guilford Press, 1991).

205   psychoanalyst D. W. Winnicott's idea . . . Winnicott viewed this shared state of being as a condition of "illusion." He distinguishes the state of unintegration from those of disintegration and integration. Unintegration is the experience of letting go, the state of feeling safe being "nobody." The expression "be nobody" from

Mark Epstein, *Going to Pieces Without Falling Apart,* New York: Broadway Books, 1998, p. 37.

Epilogue: Hearing Our Own Stories

Page

210   "My daughter at eleven . . ." Anne Sexton, from "Little Girl, My Stringbean, My Lovely Woman" in Linda Gray Sexton and Lois Ames, eds., *Anne Sexton: A Self-Portrait in Letters.* (Boston: Houghton Mifflin Company, 1977): p. 246.

212   ". . . with a dead mother I needed still . . ." Anne Sexton, Ibid., p. 424.

214   "I have read each page of my mother's voyage . . ." Anne Sexton, from "Crossing the Atlantic," Ibid., p. 156.

INDEX